TIKUN OLAM

חִקּוּן עוֹלָם

TO SPEAK ON BEHALF OF THE WORLD

TIKUN OLAM ACCORDING TO DANNY SIEGEL

by

RABBI STEVEN BAYAR
NAOMI K. EISENBERGER

ILLUSTRATIONS BY RAHEL BAYAR

KTAV PUBLISHING HOUSE INC.

Dedicated to

Blanche Bayar

A True Woman of Valor

and

Danny Siegel

Who Started it All

TABLE OF CONTENTS

To the Student:

We hope you enjoy this text/workbook. As you use it you will learn how you can change the world and be a Mitzvah Hero.

Here are some ideas about how to use this book. Each lesson is divided into three basic parts: *Texts*, *Stories of Mitzvah Heroes* and *Activities*.

- Each lesson starts with basic information about the topic. Read this carefully, as it forms the foundation of the lesson.
- Many of the lessons have a section entitled **"Texts On."** This is a group of texts that relate to the subject. Following the texts are questions on selected words in the texts. Study the questions. The next page gives you a chance to answer the questions about the selected words. Work alone, in groups or with your parents. It is our hope that you will learn from the texts of our tradition and provide your own commentary to enrich our tradition.
- Each lesson has a section entitled **"Thoughts from Danny."** We learn what Danny writes about each topic.
- Each lesson has one or two stories of **Mitzvah Heroes.** They are people who actually devote their lives to the values we are learning about. They are models to emulate.
- Finally, each lesson has a section entitled, **"Things To Do."** Unless you reinforce the values learned with actions – the lesson is not effective.
- Although Danny has always used the Ashkenazi word for *Mitzvahs,* due to the current usage in religious schools, we are using Sephardic pronunciation throughout the book.

20 percent of food in America is thrown out.

***

Only some of us can learn by other people's mistakes.
The rest of us have to be the other people.

—Anonymous

Vocabulary

Mensch: a human being
Menschen: human beings
Menschlichkeit: acting like a human being

Who is Danny Siegel?

How to begin a chapter about Danny Siegel? Danny is first and foremost a teacher of **menschen**. Danny believes that **menschlichkeit** can be taught in the classroom. He believes that any one person can make a difference in the world.

Danny believes that *learning* about doing good in the world is fine, *but* there comes a point when you have to stop *talking* about Mitzvot and start *doing* them. Danny's wish is to bring you to the point where you will say, "Yes, I can do that – Yes! I will do that!"

Danny is passionate about Tzedakah. Sometimes so passionate that he gets carried away. He tries to be positive and encouraging, but his mission is too important – and too real. When you meet the Mitzvah Heroes he works with, when you see how their work reduced hunger and pain and misery, you know that that one-dollar you give may save a life now! How can he be other than passionate? How can we?

Perhaps the greatest stumbling block confronting us is our inability to assess our own potential. In looking at developmentally disabled individuals we constantly underestimate what they are capable of. We give them pity instead of support. In much the same way, we often undervalue ourselves and our ability to achieve. If you were to ask any of the Mitzvah Heroes in this book whether they set out to change the world, they would tell you emphatically **"no."** In most cases they tried to right a wrong they saw in their own back yard.

Mitzvot Grow

Most people who give Tzedakah come to recognize that they have received more than they have given. There is magic to the act of doing Mitzvot. To many they are a way to regain a lost innocence, a loss of purity that comes naturally as we accumulate life experiences and become jaded through loss and interaction.

Mitzvot are a way of making us all more humble, as we recognize the depths of human misery around us. It can make us more more sensitive, more compassionate human beings.

The act of giving Tzedakah not only changes the life of the person in need, it can change our life as well. Who I am and what I have become is in great part molded by the great satisfaction I get when I know I have helped someone. Those who reject this process as a way of growth cannot grow.

You Can Reach Out

Tzedakah is a way of searching for meaning in life. This "meaning" can become clearer the more we engage in substantive good deeds.

There is also a sense of equality for those who work in Tzedakah fields. It doesn't matter whether you are rich, poor or somewhere in between. Whether you are healthy or ill, whether you are intelligent or developmentally disabled. Each person is capable of reaching out to those in need. Each person who does so is equal to all others who do the same and also recognizes the inherent equality of all others who reach out.

It is a curious fact of Tzedakah work that those who jump into it spontaneously, because they perceive the need and move to fix it are able to do more for longer periods of time than those who take their time and move cautiously. Motivation is a powerful force. It leads people to start programs in which they become invested. Founders of projects last longer.

Even if you are not organized, even if you stumble and find yourself muddling through, others will be attracted to you if only because of your sincerity and enthusiasm. If you find reward in your work, so will others. They will come to help you, even if only out of pity because you are so unorganized! But, they will come.

Mitzvot done poorly still have the same effect – they save lives. Before you criticize someone, first ask yourself if you are helping anyone. Chances are if you are involved in Mitzvah work, you will not criticize an enthusiastic motivated novice. Instead, you will try to teach him/her.

Tzedakah and Respect

Tzedakah must be accompanied by respect; respect for the recipient, respect for the workers, respect for the world. Humiliation detracts from Tzedakah, self-esteem raises it. One penny given with respect for the dignity of the individual does more than $100 given through humiliation. Nearly anything accomplished for the good by arrogance and high handedness can be accomplished at least as effectively by kindness and sweetness, gentleness and humility.

In this way, when we give Tzedakah, we should project ourselves into the body of the recipient. Would we want to get what we are giving? Would we eat what we are donating? This is the criterion to use.

The full impact and richness of the Tzedakah act depends on the amount of lovingkindness put into the act.
—Sukkah 49b

Tzedakah work is based on the principle of *"You just never know."*
- You never know who is really being helped: the person in need, you, or someone else you don't know.
- This is because Tzedakah has a "trickle-down" effect. When you help someone, you not only help him or her, but you show others what should be done.
- Modeling creates students.
- Students do Tzedakah.
- Acts of Tzedakah create more models and more students.

Questions

1. What type of person is Danny Siegel? _____
   _____

2. Why is Danny so passionate about Tzedakah? _____
   _____

3. List all the good things that can happen when you do Tzedakah. ___
   _____

4. Why is respect so important when doing Tzedakah? _____
   _____

5. What is the principle of Tzedakah? _____
   _____

So you see, when you perform one act of Tzedakah, the effects can be limitless.

Now you know about Danny Siegel and his Tzedakah work. One question we will ask you again and again is, **"Based upon what you have learned, what would Danny do?"**

Things to Do

1. Write a letter to Danny Siegel. Tell him what you think about Tzedakah.

2. Tell him about some of the Tzedakah projects in which you have participated.

3. Write a paper on the topic of respect. Why is respect so important? How do people show their disrespect? How can we learn to show more respect?

Here goes:

BASED UPON WHAT YOU HAVE LEARNED, WHAT WOULD DANNY DO?

_____

_____

_____

Vocabulary

Tikun Olam:
תִּקּוּן עוֹלָם
Mitzvah Hero:
גְּמִילוּת חֲסָדִים
Gemiluth Chasadim:

To fix the world

Someone who dedicates their entire life or a portion of their life to helping people in need.
Showing compassion for others.

The **Ziv Tzedakah** Fund honors those people who work tirelessly for the benefit of those in need. These people are called **Mitzvah heroes.**

In this course you are going to learn:

- About **Mitzvah heroes**. What makes them heroes? What makes them special?
- How to identify a **Mitzvah hero**.
- How to become a **Mitzvah hero**.
- About **Tzedakah**, its many forms and issues.
- Many different definitions of **Tzedakah**.
- Many stories, read about the lives of **Mitzvah heroes**, and study texts about all of these topics.

The phrase that sums up everything we hope you will learn to do is **Tikun Olam** (to fix the world). What is **Tikun Olam**? What does it mean to "fix the world"? Ask yourself this question:

What are some of the things in this world that need fixing?

One of the most troubling questions facing our tradition concerns the Creation of the world. How could God create a world that, from the very beginning, needed to be fixed?

How could a perfect God create an imperfect world?

This text tries to answer the question.

Before God created the world, there was only God. When God decided to create the world, God pulled back in order to create a space for the world. It was in that space that the universe was formed. But now, in that space, there was no God. So God created special Divine Sparks, special lights to be placed back into God's creation.

So God created the light, and placed the light inside of God's creation in special containers that were prepared to hold the light. But, there was an accident, a cosmic accident. The containers broke.

The universe became filled with sparks of God's Divine light and shards of the broken containers.

Sparks cannot shed the light the containers could. Thus our world has been deprived of the best of God's Divine light. Our tradition teaches us that one of our tasks is to gather the sparks of God's light back together. If we can repair the vessels we can again encapsulate the Divine light, restoring the world to its original intended order. In this way the work of Creation will be completed.

This act is called Tikun Olam, repairing the world.

Because it is up to us to repair the world, we have become God's partners in Creation. Together we can fix the world. We are taught that the way in which we can fix the world is to care for one another. **Gemiluth Chasadim** are actions we do that show our love and care for one another.

But before we can begin the process of **Tikun Olam**, Danny Siegel teaches us to ask some questions to guide us:

What are the other person's needs?

Then, and only then, should we ask these four questions:

What am I good at?

For example, do you play the trumpet? Can you make a salad? Do you like to draw? Do you like to watch football games? You might think that none of these activities can be put to use helping other people. You would be wrong.

Football game watchers, particularly people who like to surf the channels so they can follow three games at once, can be assigned to the home of other football lovers who used to love to surf the channels but whose hands are no longer able to.

What do I like to do?

Do you like to play the piano? Do you like to play sports? Do you like to cook? Do you like to learn about people? Do you like to talk on the phone? All of these activities can be put to good use in helping others.

If you like to talk, think about talking to residents of a nursing home, of getting to know them, telling them about yourself—and learning about them as well. If you like to cook (whether you are good at it or not), think of putting those skills to good use cooking for a soup kitchen.

Whom do I know?

Chances are you know a lot of people with skills or resources that can be used to help people in need. Your fiends have many talents. Parents have jobs that can be used to help others as well.

Why not (help others)?

After all of this, ask the question, "What is keeping you from helping others?"
The answer is **probably 'nothing.'**

PERSONAL INVENTORY

Whom do I know?	What skills do they have?	How can these skills help others?

FILL OUT THE FOLLOWING CHART

What am I good at?	How can I use this skill to help others?	Where can I do it?

For more than a dozen years I have been obsessed with the **Mitzvah of Tzedakah,** exploring the Jewish mode of giving from many different perspectives. I have tried to get the "feel" of Tzedakah by establishing a non-profit organization called **Ziv Tzedakah Fund....**

Of late, I have turned to **Mitzvah Heroes**, those captivating people who draw you into their circle so powerfully and yet, more often than not, so gently. My purpose in recording some aspects of their lives and Mitzvah work is a most practical one: I would like people to read this book and say, "Oh, I must meet these people, work with them, do something."

I want my readers to meet the heroes and listen to them and ask questions:

How did you start?

Why did you start?

What keeps you going?

How much does this interfere with the rest of your life?

Where do you get the time and energy and faith to do so much?

How can I do some of this?

Munbaz II, p. 3

Questions

1. What is the Ziv Tzedakah Fund? _____
_____

2. Why was it set up? _____
_____

3. Why does Danny Siegel write about **Mitzvah Heroes**? _____
_____

Everyone needs teachers. We need geography teachers—people who know maps and places, distances, the kinds of people who live in cities or in the countryside. History teachers are women and men who read and study how the world has passed from one generation to another—why some events and some leaders have changed things so much that the world is never the same. Science teachers show us why things fall to the ground, how human beings were able to land on the moon, why, when you throw some cocoa powder into milk and stir it, it comes out thick and creamy and tasty.

We need teachers in Tzedakah, too

They are at least as important as our history, geography, and science teachers. They work with us to teach us how to take whatever money we have, and whatever talents and energy we have, and to make them do the most **Tikun Olam.**

Dr. Eliezer Jaffe is one of the best Tzedakah teachers in the world. Born in America, he moved to Israel more than twenty years ago. A social worker, he became a professor of social work at Hebrew University in Jerusalem. He has taught thousands of students how to understand what's right and what's not so right about Israeli society, and how to fix what is not so right. No one knows better than Dr. Jaffe how one person or a few people, or many people working together, can make Israel (and any society) a better place to live. He knows and understands "grass-roots Tzedakah" so well that he has organized many groups that have made a difference. His most famous one is the Israel Free Loan Society, which has loaned millions of dollars to people in need at no charge and

no extra costs when the people repay the loan. "Free loan" means exactly that: they lend out money at no cost.

Dr. Jaffe understands how people can get the government to change laws so that life is better: for immigrants, for large families, for people with disabilities, for people who want to adopt children.

There are many amazing things about Dr. Jaffe. He knows a tremendous number of facts and numbers about people in Israel. He "gets" it—which means not only that he know the facts, but that he knows how to use this knowledge to make things better. And, most amazing is that he speaks very softly. You might think someone like this would have a booming voice and might be pushy or overbearing. Not so. He says things that make so much sense, you see how right he is, and you join him in his work to make life an experience filled with caring.

Yes, a great teacher, someone we can learn from, someone who can show us what we can do and who we can be if we use our talent and money wisely for **Tikun Olam.**

Questions

1. Why do we need teachers? _____
_____

2. What kind of teacher is Eliezer Jaffe? _____
_____

3. What is his profession? _____
_____

4. What does a teacher like Eliezer Jaffe have to do with Tikun Olam? _____
_____

5. Where does Eliezer Jaffe live? _____
_____

6. Why does Dr. Jaffe know better than most people how to help people in Israel? _____
_____
_____

Can't Be Failed Exam:

	YES	NO

1. Did you visit a hospital this year?

2. If so, did you bring smiles to the faces of those you visited?

3. Did you plant a tree in Israel this year?

4. Is Tzedakah something you think about?

5. How many Tzedakah programs did you contribute to this year?

6. Is there a food bin in your congregation?

7. Are there large-print prayerbooks in your congregation?

8. Is there a Tzedakah box in your house?

9. How many times this year has the Tzedakah box been filled?

10. Did you buy gifts for needy people on Chanukah?

11. Did you give Tzedakah on your birthday?

12. How many developmentally different children or adults know your name?

13. Have you visited a nursing home this year?

14. Do you buy an extra item of food for Tzedakah when grocery shopping?

15. Does your congregation donate leftover food to shelters?

16. Have you been to a soup kitchen this year?

17. Have you been to a food bank this year?

18. Does your congregation have a handicapped-accessible bathroom?

19. Does your congregation have a handicapped-accessible water fountain?

20. Does your congregation have a ramp and accessible entrance?

21. Can someone in a wheelchair get onto the bimah?

22. Does your congregation have a teletypewriter phone?

23. Does your congregation have a special sound system for the hard of hearing?

	YES	NO
24. Does your congregation have Braille prayerbooks? 24.		
25. Does your congregation have Braille Bibles? 25.		
26. Have you visited a group home in your area? 26.		
27. Did you take part in a clothing drive this year? 27.		
28. Did you take part in a food drive this year? 28.		
29. Has your school or congregation visited a nursing home this year? 29.		
30. How many books are in your Tzedakah library? 30.		
31. Has your family given blood this year? 31.		
32. Have members of your family had their bone marrow tested so that they might be possible donors for someone with leukemia? 32.		
33. What is the name of the nearest food bank? 33.		
34. Is there a local shelter for victims of domestic violence? 34.		
35. Do you know how to contact that shelter? 35		

Things to Do

1. Talk to your parents, your relatives, and friends. Ask them if they know anyone who qualifies as a **Mitzvah Hero.**

2. Fill in the following chart. Use the information they give you.

3. **Write a letter to Danny Siegel, c/o Ziv, 384 Wyoming Avenue, Millburn, New Jersey, 07041.**

   Send him the chart you have completed on Mitzvah Heroes.

Name of Mitzvah Hero	Name given to me by	What do they do?

Vocabulary

If you were to look up the word "Hero" and the word "Celebrity" in a dictionary, you would find the following definitions:

Hero:
חַיָל

A person admired for their achievements and accomplishments. A person who shows great courage.

Celebrity:
מְפֻרְסָם

A person who is widely known and referred to often.

There is a difference between someone who is gifted with special abilities and someone who is "put to the test." Many people listed as heroes (rock stars, actors, actresses and sports figures) are able to do things that the rest of us may only dream of, but that does not make them heroes.

A hero is judged by his or her effect upon others. They are not judged by their ability or popularity. Could a hero be someone in a wheelchair? Could a hero be unattractive? If your answer to these two questions is "no," then you may not understand what makes a person a hero.

Of course, there are people who are both stars and heroes. Which do you think is the more important of the two?

How would you interpret the following saying?
Good leaders make us think, "Oh, if only I could do that, be like that."
Great leaders make us think, "If they can do that, then…I can too."

List four of your heroes in the chart below:

Name of Your Hero	What Does He/She Do?	Why Is He/She Your Hero?

It all started with a seemingly endless scream coming from a nearby apartment. Only someone in great pain could be crying out like that. Then a young woman, Bracha Kapach, went to investigate. What she found astounded her. In a dirty, meagerly furnished room in her poor Jerusalem neighborhood, lay a woman crying out in pain. Sick from hunger, the woman wanted only one thing—to die. And so began the long and amazing work of the Rabbanit Kapach (she is called "Rabbanit" because her husband was a Rabbi), now a legend in Israel. With love and kindness, the Rabbanit nursed this woman back to health, providing her not only with sustenance for her body but love and respect for her soul.

Today, the Rabbanit's work is known throughout the country. The State of Israel has even awarded her the Israel Prize, the highest honor that can be bestowed upon a private individual in that country.

Her work knows no bounds. Jerusalem is a city filled with many, many poor people. If you sit in her living room on a Friday morning you will see a seemingly endless stream of visitors searching for some special food for the coming Shabbat. Kugels, fresh fruit, a package of rice, some pita bread, whatever it takes to make Shabbat special. Others help the Rabbanit with her work by preparing food or offering money to supplement her expenses.

Before Pesach, the Rabbanit enlists a crew of volunteers who help her prepare thousands of food packages filled with rice, oil, sugar, and matzot. The distribution of the more than 4000 packages requires the closing of local streets, the use of a nearby school and hundreds of hours of donated manpower, not to mention the cost—more than $25,000 (all of which is paid by private donations

which do not always cover the total costs and frequently leaves the Rabbanit in debt.)

In the summer months, the Rabbanit's day camp provides fun and play for many children who would otherwise be left to play on the city's hot, dusty streets. The kids are treated to games, swimming and an occasional tiyul (field trip) to break up the long days. For mothers, frequently burdened by the stresses of raising large families in the midst of poverty, the Rabbanit even offers swimming classes which provide a welcome respite from the heat and noise of the city.

The Rabbanit Kapach is under no illusions. She knows that the people she helps, in many cases, need much more than she can provide. However, she believes that small acts of kindness can multiply. She doesn't judge the people who come to her. She helps them.

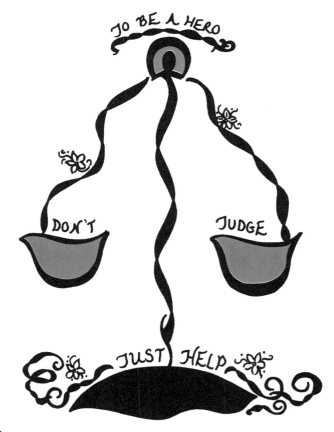

22

Questions on the Rabbanit Kapach:

1. Who is the Rabbanit Kapach? _____

2. How did she get started as a Mitzvah Hero? _____

3. Why was she awarded the Israel Prize? _____

4. What is Friday morning like in the Rabbanit's apartment? _____

5. What does the Rabbanit do before Pesach? _____

6. How does the Rabbanit treat each person she helps with respect? _____

7. How doe the Rabbanit contribute to Tikun Olam? _____

8. Would you call the Rabbanit a "Hero" or a "Celebrity?" Why? _____

Things To Do:

1. For the next class, tell about one of your heroes. If available, bring in any news articles about him/her.

2. Ask your parents to list their five "heroes." For the next class, compare all the parents' lists with yours.

3. If you could invite any two people, living or deceased, past, present or future, real or fictional, to a Shabbat meal, who would they be?

4. Have some newspapers and magazines at hand. Look through them to see if you can spot some real heroes. Read the story about them and discuss why these people qualify as heroes.

5. Ask the Rabbi, Cantor or principal to tell the class about their heroes.

6. Make a list of what it would take to prepare a "Shabbat Kit" for a family in need. Explain?

7. Make up five "Shabbat Kits" and donate them to the Jewish Family Service in your area.

BASED UPON WHAT YOU HAVE LEARNED, WHAT WOULD DANNY DO?

_____

_____

_____

Part I: Our Story

As we talk about the concepts of **"Celebrity"** and **"Hero"** it is important to learn to tell the difference between the two. How can you recognize **"Heroes"** in your community? How do you find them? As we study these texts from our tradition and learn about **Mitzvah Heroes**, keep an eye out for someone who might qualify as one. In Hebrew we translate "Mitzvah Hero" as "Ba'al Tzedakah," a "master of Tzedakah."
How would you interpret the following teaching?

There are two seas in the Land of Israel.
One is fresh and fish are in it.
Splashes of green are on its shores.
Trees spread their branches over it and
Stretch out their thirsty roots to sip of its waters.
Along its shore children play.
The other has no fish.
No trees grow alongside it.
No one lives nearby.
The air hangs heavy above its waters and
Its waters are undrinkable.
What is the difference?
The Sea of Galilee receives water from the Jordan River, but does not keep it.
Giving and receiving go on in equal measure.
The other receives but gives nothing away.
That is why it is called the Dead Sea

WHAT CAN YOU THINK OF ??

Questions:

1. What are the two bodies of water described? _____

_____

2. What is the difference between them? _____

_____

3. How does this story liken the bodies of water to people? _____

_____

4. What is the message of the story? _____

_____

Part II:

Text On Tzedakah

Perhaps the most important book of Jewish Law is called the Shulchan Aruch, which means "the set table." This text is taken from this Code of Jewish Law.

Stay Far Away from Needing Tzedakah

> A person should try as hard as possible not to need Tzedakah…Even a scholar who is honored should work in crafts rather than accept funds….Anyone who needs to take money and cannot live without it should take it: i.e. an aged person, or a sick person…If he doesn't take the funds this is like murder and he is responsible for his own life.
>
> ***Yoreh Deah: 255***

Questions

1. Why should we try hard not to need Tzedakah? _____

2. What does it mean to "work in crafts?" _____

3. Why would the texts tell us that it is better to "work in crafts" than accept funds? _____

4. What happens if you really need Tzedakah but refuse to take it? _____

5. Is it possible for a hero to accept Tzedakah? How? _____

Around the town of Columbia, South Carolina, everyone knows John Fling as the "Everyday Santa." If he walks into a local restaurant, the manager will start packing up food in take-out containers. John Fling knows someone who could use that extra meal. In the supermarket it is the same story—when John comes in they know that he will want some cans and boxes of food to take to someone who is just getting by with barely enough to eat.

John was born around 1908. He was raised in a sharecropper's house in Gabbettville, Georgia, population about 45 people. Eighteen of those people were his brothers and sisters. John claims that having such a large family taught him how to share, and share he does.

Though retired from his full-time job, he is still active. Rising early each morning, John makes his rounds of the area taking care of three kinds of people: children, people who are blind, and just about anyone else who finds him or whom he finds. In this part of South Carolina many people are poor—very poor.

How does John help these people? He helps them in every possible way. The city has given him a special permit to set up a "clothes sale" (for free) anywhere he wants. Just like that he strings up a heavy cord against a tree or telephone pole, and people come to take what they need—no strings attached (except, maybe, to the tree or pole).

Stories about Fling are the stuff of legends. He once had a group of his blind friends paint an old man's shack. His friends felt good about helping, for it is not often that a blind person gets to help someone else. The old man, wheelchair-bound, got his one-room shack painted and everyone had fun.

Another time, he went to the supermarket with a blind friend who needed to buy dog food for her pet. When the clerk at the checkout would not sell her the food for her seeing eye dog because her food stamps only covered food for humans, John jumped into action. Right in front of the manager, John opened the bag of dog food and started eating, proving that it was fit for humans. The store still refused to accept the food stamps for the dog food but John's friend got the bag for free. There was another time he got a color TV for a blind girl. Why a color TV? Because the sound is better on newer models of televisions. The social service agency wanted to deduct the cost of the TV from the girl's monthly support check. Fling gathered some reporters and news people, picked up the TV and brought it to the social service office. The media had a field day.

A good part of John's day, though, is spent just driving around and talking to people. He listens to their problems and tries to help as much as he can. He is not an "easy mark," though. One man asked John if he would pay to fix his broken lawnmower. Rather than pay, John brought the man a repair manual and now the man has a business fixing lawn mowers.

If you go down John Fling's way on Sunday morning, you will see him in his van, picking kids up to go to church, with perhaps a stop at the local doughnut shop.

John Fling considers his a "most blessed life" because he can spend it helping others.

Questions about John Fling:

1. Where does John Fling live? _____

2. What is an average day for John Fling? _____

3. Why is he well known in his hometown? _____

4. What kind of "legends" have been told about John? _____

5. Would you say that John is a "celebrity" in his hometown? Why or why not? _____

6. Would you say that John is a "hero" in his hometown? Why? _____

BASED UPON WHAT YOU HAVE LEARNED, WHAT WOULD DANNY DO?

_____

_____

_____

_____

Vocabulary:

Brit/Covenant: בְּרִית	A contract, an agreement between two parties. The word Covenant is used to describe the very special relationship between God and the Jewish people.

Why should we begin this class about Tzedakah by talking about Brit? In order to understand what Judaism teaches about the concept of Tzedakah it is important to learn why Tzedakah is so meaningful to Jewish life and belief.

There are many different ways of looking at the relationship between God and the Jewish people. The purpose of this lesson is to show you some of the different ways we view God, interpret the Torah and celebrate Judaism. What we think of the Brit helps form our identity as Jews.

Each movement of Judaism believes that we are a Covenant People. But just as each movement understands God's relationship to us and the source of Torah differently, each views Covenant differently. What you believe about the source of Torah determines what you believe about the nature of our Covenant with God. Our tradition has existed for thousands of years. In that time we have developed differing ways of viewing God and God's relationship with us.

Sometimes people share a common language but still do not understand each other. Two people can look at the same sentence and understand it differently. For example: What does this sentence mean?

He is not guilty.

1. Can you think of more than one way to interpret this sentence?

_____

2. How do these interpretations differ?

_____

3. Can you see how two people interpreting this phrase in different ways, could disagree on some very fundamental issues?

_____

4. Can you think of other situations where two people can read the same sentence and understand it differently?

_____

5. How then would you interpret this sentence?
"We have a relationship with God that is based upon the Brit."

_____

6. Almost every word in this sentence can be interpreted in different ways.

_____

What does "we" mean? Does it mean:

Members of our family?

_____

Friends?

_____

Jews?

_____

Non-Jews?

_____

Americans?

_____

Animals?

_____

Different people interpret this phrase in different ways. Would a vegetarian agree with a meat-eater? There have been many examples in our history where the word "we" excluded more people than it did include! For example, the Constitution of the United States of America begins with the phrase, "We the people…" yet did not include African-Americans in the guarantee of freedom.

What does the word "relationship" mean? Does it mean

- A family relationship?

- A business relationship?

- A friendly relationship?

Is your relationship with your teacher the same kind of relationship as with your parents? Is it the same as the one you have with your friends? How are they different? In some relationships we as individuals are more central, in some we are less central. Relationships can be complicated and varied.

What does the word "God" mean? There are many different ideas and perceptions about God. What kind of relationship does the word "Covenant" mean?

While we can discuss the meaning of these words forever, one thing about any **"Covenant"** is clear. Any relationship based upon a **Covenant** has, at its core, the fact that while both sides enter into the agreement voluntarily, from the time they agree and "sign on the dotted line," it is binding on both sides.

There are several **Covenants** mentioned in the Torah. When God creates the world God establishes a **Covenant** with Adam, Eve and all of Creation. The "sign" of this contract is called "Shabbat." When the flood destroys all life except for Noah and those in the Ark, God agrees never to destroy the world again through water. The sign of this **Covenant** is the rainbow. When Abraham becomes the first person to accept a **Covenant** with God, the token of this relationship is called circumcision.

In the **Covenant** between God and Israel described in the Torah, we agree to remain loyal to God and God promises to protect the people and find them a homeland.

Fill Out the Following Table:

Relationship	My Responsibility To Them	Their Responsibility To Me
My Parents – Myself		
My Friends – Myself		
My Teachers – Myself		
My God – Myself		
My Pets – Myself		
My Friends – Myself		
My Doctor – Myself		

Texts on Brit/Covenant

In this section, you will study texts from our tradition about the topic in the lesson. Read the texts. Under the text are questions about certain words (in bold) in the texts. Read the questions and discuss them. Feel free to ask other questions about the texts.

The heaven and the earth were **finished**. On the seventh day God finished the work that He had been doing, and He ceased on the seventh day from **all the work** that He had done. God **blessed** the seventh day and declared it **holy**, because on it God ceased from all the work of creation that He had done. Such is the story of heaven and earth when they were created   *(Genesis 2:1-4)…*

God spoke to (Avram) further, "As for Me, this is My Covenant with you: You shall be the **father of a multitude of nations**. You shall no longer be called Avram, but your name shall be **Avraham**…I will maintain My Covenant between Me and you, and your **offspring to come**, as an everlasting Covenant throughout the ages, to be God to you and to your offspring…I assign **the land** you live in to you and your offspring to come…an everlasting holding. I will be their God. As for you, you and your offspring to come shall keep My Covenant…every male among you shall be **circumcised**…at the age of eight days   *(Genesis 17:4-12)…*

When God finished speaking with him (Moses) on Mount Sinai, He gave Moses the **two tablets of the Agreement**, stone tablets inscribed with the finger of God   *(Exodus 31:18)…*

Finished: What does it mean to be "finished?" (Tikun Olam) All the work: Why does the text tell us many times how "God finished working." Is there some hidden meaning to this?

Blessed: What does it mean to "bless" a day? How is it made "holy?"

Father of a multitude of nations: What nations? What does it mean to be a "father" to all the nations?

Avraham: Why must Avraham's name be changed for the Covenant?

Offspring to come: Why does God mention Avraham's children and descendants in this Covenant?

The land: Why is land so important to the Covenant?

Circumcised: Why is it so important to be circumcised?

Two tablets of the agreement: What are these tablets? Why are they called the "tablets of the agreement?"

Texts on Brit/Covenant

On this page, write your interpretations (and answers) to the questions raised here or in discussion. In this way you will develop your own guide to Mitzvot!

The heaven and the earth were **finished**. On the seventh day God finished the work that He had been doing, and He ceased on the seventh day from **all the work** that He had done. God **blessed** the seventh day and declared it **holy**, because on it God ceased from all the work of creation that He had done. Such is the story of heaven and earth when they were created   *(Genesis 2:1-4)...*

God spoke to (Avram) further, "As for Me, this is My Covenant with you: You shall be the **father of a multitude of nations**. You shall no longer be called Avram, but your name shall be **Avraham**...I will maintain My Covenant between Me and you, and your **offspring to come**, as an everlasting Covenant throughout the ages, to be God to you and to your offspring...I assign **the land** you live in to you and your offspring to come...an everlasting holding. I will be their God. As for you, you and your offspring to come shall keep My Covenant...every male among you shall be **circumcised**...at the age of eight days   *(Genesis 17:4-12)...*

When God finished speaking with him (Moses) on Mount Sinai, He gave Moses the **two tablets of the Agreement**, stone tablets inscribed with the finger of God
(Exodus 31:18)...

Finished: _____

_____

Blessed: _____

Father of a multitude of nations: _____

Avraham: _____

Offspring to come: _____

The land: _____

Circumcised: _____

Two tablets of the agreement: _____

Thoughts from Danny Siegel

Consider the situation in Montreal, Canada. After a demographic study, the Jewish community discovered there were 10,000 of its 90,000 Jews living in poverty. After their initial astonishment at the magnitude of the human needs, the members of the Jewish community immediately put enormous efforts and talents toward finding solutions to this devastating situation. No one blamed the victims, the poor Jews, no one recited the standard list of woes, "We are already overwhelmed with work" or, "Where shall we find the resources?" Foremost in the minds of the leaders in Montreal was the benefit of their poor Jewish brothers and sisters.

Good People, p. 157

Questions:

1. What percentage of Jews living in Montreal were living in poverty? _____

   _____

2. Why would the Jewish community in Montreal be astonished by this? _____

   _____

3. Why would anyone "blame the victims" in a situation like this?_____

   _____

4. What reasons would people give for not wanting to help the poor people?_____

   _____

5. Why did the Jews of Montreal decide to help?_____

   _____

He pronounces his name "Yo-ayl," even though it is spelled "Yöel" And he knows better than most people what it means to start all over again, to come to a new home, to settle in and make a new life.

When he was a child growing up in Germany, the Nazis came to power and began their evil campaign that we came to know as the Shoah—he destruction of the Jews of Europe. His family ran away, crossing many borders to escape. (He would have had a formal Bar Mitzvah, but he was in prison in Spain.) Eventually—before 1948 when Israel was born—he arrived safely in Israel and fought in the War of Independence. After that, he settled on a Kibbutz called Palmach Tzuba outside of Jerusalem, where he still lives as a Kibbutznik. The Palmach was a special army that defended the Jews in Israel before 1948 and fought to make the country free. The Kibbutz was started by Palmach-niks. Finally, Yöel was home, a free man, no longer afraid for his life.

Besides being a regular Kibbutznik doing what a Kibbutznik does—driving tractors, working in the glass factory, planting and harvesting crops—he has a special job: he is the director of the Ya'akov Maimon Volunteers. Somewhere along the way he met Ya'akov Maimon, a man who organized people to go all over Israel to help immigrants learn Hebrew and to work with them to adjust to this new home of theirs. Thousands of people have been Maimon Volunteers, and when Ya'akov Maimon died in the 1960's, Yöel took over, to make sure the work would continue. Yoel wants the people from the former Soviet Union, from Ethiopia, from wherever they may have come, to settle in and be happy. He understands what they are going through.

Yöel understands that the Nazis tried to kill the Jews for no other reason than that they were Jews. He understands that Israel is a special place, a homeland promised to the Jews, a safe place to be. It isn't clear exactly how he understands God in the last 60 or 70 years of Jewish history, but he knows that the Jewish people have a special place in history, building and rebuilding their lives and the Land of Israel is what he should be doing. There's some special agreement—a Brit, a Covenant—that ties it all together. Something inside of him—maybe a voice which we might call The Voice of God—says he has to do it. It just has to be done, this is what Jews are supposed to be doing.

Even his name tells us that: in Germany, the family name was "Dispecker." Then it was changed to "Dorkam," which is Hebrew for "A generation arises." He is part of those new generations that make Jewish history something new and better every day. . . including many grandchildren of his own.

Questions about Yöel Dorkam:

1. Where did Yöel grow up? _____

2. Why did he leave his homeland? _____

3. Where would his Bar Mitzvah have been? Why? _____

4. Where does Yöel live now? _____

5. What is his job? _____

6. What else does he do? _____

7. Who was Ya'akov Maimon and what did he do? _____

8. What does Yöel's helping others have to do with the Brit/Covenant? _____
_____

BASED UPON WHAT YOU HAVE LEARNED, WHAT WOULD DANNY DO?

_____
_____
_____
_____
_____
_____
_____
_____
_____
_____
_____

Vocabulary:

Mitzvah:
מִצְוָה

There are two definitions of **Mitzvah**; a commandment, something you "must" do, or something we do in response to what we believe God wants of us.

Many people think that a **Mitzvah** is a good deed. It certainly is. However the word **"Mitzvah"** is not defined in that way. It means so much more. A **Mitzvah** is something we do in response to what we believe God wants of us. Some **Mitzvot** are done with a group, others are done alone. Tzedakah is a **Mitzvah**.

As in the word **Brit**, different groups of Jews have differing ideas about the Mitzvot we perform. Just like the word **Brit**, the way each movement interprets this word helps define what that movement is.

Many people believe that the concept of **Mitzvah** is used to help us learn what it means to be Jewish. Having a set of actions that the Torah teaches us to do helps us learn what Jews do. Just as athletes have to train hard to become professional baseball players, football players or ice skaters, just as becoming a scientist means training hard to learn all the things a scientist must know, just like becoming good at anything means working hard to learn what it takes to accomplish your goal, the **Mitzvot** help us learn how to become good Jews.

It would be nice to believe that on their own everyone would be merciful and kind to others because they wanted to, but people are not that way. The **Mitzvot** serve to teach what is expected of us and how we are to achieve these goals, so that we have an easier time succeeding.

In order to follow the laws of the Torah we need to have a
- Common understanding of what is expected of us.
- Common effort
- Common identity for all involved.

We must all be "on the same page." For example, when we light Shabbat candles, we light them in our own homes – but everyone is lighting Shabbat candles together, at the same time, all over the world. This is the power of **Mitzvot**. In this way we can learn how to feed hungry people, observe Shabbat, pray, treat others with respect.

Tzedakah is an example of a **Mitzvah** that can support and strengthen the community. Because of the **Mitzvah** of Tzedakah, our community has a common understanding of what is expected of us. It takes individual people to perform the acts of Tzedakah, but to provide for many people it takes a community effort. Acts of Tzedakah bind us together in bonds of common purpose.

A **Mitzvah** requires action. The more Mitzvot we do, the better people we become.

Fill in the chart below:

Texts About	What Does It Mean To Me?	What I Have To Do About It
You shall each revere his mother and father and keep My Sabbaths: I am Adonai your God. *Leviticus 19:3*		
You Shall not pick your vineyard bare, or gather the fallen fruit of your vineyard; you shall leave them for the poor and the stranger, I Adonai am your God. *Leviticus 19:10*		
You shall not insult the deaf, or place a stumbling block before the blind. You shall fear your God: I am Adonai. *Leviticus 19:14*		
The stranger who resides with you shall be to you as one of your citizens; you shall love him as yourself, for you were strangers in the land of Egypt: I Adonai am your God. *Leviticus 19:34*		
You shall not boil a kid in its mother's milk. *Deuteronomy 14:21*		
There shall be no needy among you – since Adonai your God will bless you in the land which Adonai your God is giving you as a hereditary portion. If only you heed Adonai your God and take care to keep all this instruction that I enjoin you this day. *Leviticus 15:4*		

Texts on Mitzvah

For what does it matter to the Holy One Blessed be He whether or not the Jews carry out the laws of Kashrut? **It is clear** then that the commandments were given solely for the purpose of **training** the people. *(Tanchuma, Shmini 7)*…

The Mitzvot were given in order to **refine** human beings
(Vayikra Rabba 13:3)…

It is better to perform a Mitzvah than to light a candle **before God**
(Shemot Rabbah 37:3)…

What does it matter: Why should God, the Creator of all the universe, care whether we keep Mitzvot? Why should God care if we do Kiddush? Why should God care if we give Tzedakah to needy people?

It is clear: To whom is it clear? How is it clear? Who made it clear?

Training: Who is in training? What are we in training for? Why are we in training?

Refine: Why are we being refined? For what purpose? Who is refining us?

Before God: How can it be better to perform a Mitzvah than be before God? How is this possible? Why would anyone teach this?

Texts on Mitzvah

For what does it matter to the Holy One Blessed be He whether or not the Jews carry out the laws of Kashrut? **It is clear** then that the commandments were given solely for the purpose of **training** the people. *(Tanchuma, Shmini 7)*…

The Mitzvot were given in order to **refine** human beings
(Vayikra Rabba 13:3)…

It is better to perform a Mitzvah than to light a candle **before God**
(Shemot Rabbah 37:3)…

What does it matter: _____

_____

It is clear: _____

Training: _____

Refine: _____

Before God: _____

Thoughts From Danny Siegel

When Eyal was four years old, he was diagnosed with a brain tumor and the prognosis was very bleak. It was Purim day…

Eyal uses a wheelchair and needs a respirator. He has tutors and attendants. Beyond that, there is no need for details other than to say that I am grateful he sent me a copy of his Bar Mitzvah speech – and gave me permission to reprint it…

This is what Eyal said on the day he assumed full command of his Life of **Mitzvahs**.
"Shabbat Shalom!
Some people never thought I would have a Bar Mitzvah because I'm in a wheelchair and on a respirator. But this day proves them wrong! You might think this day is like a miracle, when something happens that you don't expect. Here I am today on the bimah, an honor and a pleasure to be where my father stands every week. I prepared for my Bar Mitzvah at home for a long time, starting when I was very young. I've learned to say the kiddush, blessing over the wine, and Birchat Hamazon, Grace After Meals. My family builds a Sukkah and we put on our ski jackets and eat in it. I learned the prayers by coming to services every Shabbat with my family. It was harder for me to prepare than other kids. The Cantor had to learn to read my lips. Having my Bar Mitzvah means I am a man and now my father can call me on the phone to help make up the minyan when they are short…

Bar Mitzvah Speech
Eyal Sherman
Good People, p. 19

Questions:

1.   What are Eyal's disabilities? _____

_____

2.   What does a Bar Mitzvah mean to Eyal? _____

_____

3.   What can we learn about doing Mitzvot from Eyal? _____

_____

4.   How does becoming a Bar Mitzvah impact on Eyal's dignity? _____

_____

Years ago, when Reb Osher Freund was a young man it was not an easy job trying to find him as he made his way through Jerusalem's many neighborhoods. Reb Osher was a busy man. Tzedakah was his life.

Though now older in years and in ill health many remember him as big and tall, and as, perhaps, the most gentle man they had ever met. Even today, he radiates gentleness, so much so, that in his presence you know you are standing near a holy man.

At a very young age, Reb Osher (as he later became known) would deliver fruits and vegetables to needy people. From this very first Mitzvah activity has grown today free dental clinics, Shabbat food packages, housing for poor people, catered weddings, day care centers, warm meals for elderly people, discount supermarkets, sheltered workshops for individuals with mental disabilities and a special education facility. And if all of that were not enough - consider grants to poor brides, Passover packages, free loans and tons and tons of surplus fruits and vegetables.

Reb Osher is one person on a very short list of "Tzedakah geniuses," people of great vision who have the remarkable talent of turning their vision into reality. When you meet him you learn the true meaning of doing "all that anyone can possibly do."

Yad Ezra, the name of Reb Osher's project, is an institution in Jerusalem. Thousands of people lead better lives because of his efforts. Despite the tremendous scope of his work, Reb Osher teaches his huge corps of volunteers how to work without tension, with a gentle and loving touch.

Although he himself is part of the ultra-Orthodox community, Reb Osher transcends all boundaries between Jews. No one is turned away.

BE A HERO....
Give a gift

Questions on Reb Osher Freund:

1. How would you describe Reb Osher Freund? _____

2. What Mitzvot does Reb Osher do? _____

3. What is Yad Ezra? _____

4. How does Reb Osher treat others with dignity? _____

Things To Do

1. Take a tour of the synagogue. As you go through the building, list what Mitzvot can be performed in different places. Make and fill in the following chart:

Place	Mitzvah	Who Does It?	Purpose?
Sanctuary			
Chapel			
Lobby			
School			
Parking Lot			
Social Hall			
Hallways			
Bathrooms			
Synagogue Office			
Playground			
Kitchen			

2. Take a similar tour of your home. Fill in a similar chart.

3. Read the story, "His Name was Hyam," in the book, *Who Knows Ten* (Molly Cone, Union of American Hebrew Congregations), and discuss what compelled Hyam to save a life when offered no reward and to refuse to take a life when offered a great reward.

4. Go through the exercise in Bernard Reisman's, *The New Jewish Experiential Book* on page 412, "Encounter with Jewish Ritual Objects." Include a Tzedakah box in the objects.

5. Have a personal Mitzvah day. See how many Mitzvot you can do.

BASED UPON WHAT YOU HAVE LEARNED, WHAT WOULD DANNY DO?

_____

_____

_____

_____

_____

_____

_____

_____

_____

_____

_____

_____

Vocabulary:

Covenant Community: A community tied together through its unique relationship
קָהָל   with God

List five regular activities you take part in. In what activities are you part of a community?
In which activities are you not part of a community?

Community Activity	Are You Part Of A Community?	Which Community?
Taking out the garbage	Yes	My family
Watching Television	No	I do it alone

In the previous lessons we learned about the concepts of **Brit** and **Mitzvah**. We learned that **Mitzvahs** are things we do because of our belief and acceptance of the Brit. Different forms of Judaism may have different ways of interpreting both terms, but we all accept that these words are important in shaping our Jewish selves and the way we interact with the world.

Both **Brit** and **Mitzvot** fulfill an important function in our lives. They help us create and identify our community.

Texts on Two Bible Stories

Let us look at two stories from the Torah and compare the attitudes of the main characters in each story.

Cain and Abel:

Cain and Abel are the first two children of Adam and Eve. They both brought sacrifices to God, Cain's was rejected…

Cain spoke to his brother Abel. When they were in the field, Cain rose over his brother Abel and killed him. God said to Cain, "Where is your brother Abel?"" He said, "I don't know. Am I my brother's keeper?"   *Genesis 4:8-9*

Joseph and His Brothers

Joseph was his father's (Jacob) favorite child. Jacob gave Joseph a many-colored coat to show how important he was. When Joseph began dreaming of how superior he was to his brothers, they kidnapped him and sold him as a slave down to Egypt. There, Joseph eventually succeeded, becoming the second most powerful man in all of Egypt. During a famine, when Joseph's brothers were forced to come to Egypt to buy food, Joseph found them and tested their loyalty to each other, and to see whether they were sorry for what they had done to him. All this time though, Joseph never revealed to his brothers his true identity. When it was clear that the brothers were changed men…

Joseph could no longer control himself in front of those who stood with him. He called, "Let all before me leave." No one stood with him w hen he identified himself to his brothers. He raised his voice in tears. Egypt heard. The house of Pharaoh heard. Joseph said to his brothers, "I am Joseph, is my father yet alive?" His brothers could not answer him because they were afraid of him. Joseph said to his brothers, "Come close to me." They did. He said, "I am Joseph your brother whom you sold down to Egypt. Do not be worried or angry that you sold me here, for God sent me here to keep us alive…"

Genesis 45:1-5

What are some of the differences between Cain and Joseph?

Joseph	Cain

The differences between Cain and Joseph tells us a lot about what a community should be. Joseph sees himself as part of a community - his family. It is a community founded upon the Brit between God and Abraham. Thus, even when he is sold as a slave by his brothers he still feels a strong tie and, more importantly, a responsibility, for the welfare of his brothers. He saves them, not because of who they are, but in spite of their previous actions. He does this because he accepts his role in the community.

Cain's case is different. He does not see himself as anything but an individual. By killing Abel he shows a lack of responsibility towards others. Cain's punishment will be to become what he is. He is forced to wander alone in the land, until he dies.

Community is one of the most important concepts in Judaism. Communities are bound together by common interest and common goals. They have common histories and share a common present. They look forward to a common future. They care for one another. As Jews we belong to a **Covenant Community.**

How does the following story explain the idea of Covenant Community?

Some people were sitting in a ship when one of them took a drill and began to bore a hole under his seat. The other passengers protested to him, "What are you doing?"

He said to them, "What has this to do with you? Am I not boring a hole under my own seat?" They retorted, "But the water will come in and drown us all."

Vayikra Rabba 4:6

How would you interpret the following texts?

Do not separate yourself from the community.
Pirke Avot 2:4

All Israel are responsible for each other.
Shevuot 39

All Israel are brothers.
Tanhuma Naso 3

The contrary child (of the Haggadah) excludes himself from the community.
Mekhilta 13:8

1. Why is this child called "contrary?" _____

_____

2. What is required of us to be the opposite of the "contrary child?" _____

_____

3. How can this be accomplished? _____

_____

4. How would you interpret the following text? _____

_____

Whoever can stop the people of their city from sinning but does not...is held responsible for the sins of the people of their city. If he can stop the whole world from sinning and does not, they are held responsible for the sins of the whole world.

Shabbat 54b

Thoughts from Danny Siegel:

This is the story of one trip a few months ago, and it is a relatively simple story—once you think about it…As the weekend developed it became clear that this particular congregation was ready for some more extraordinary (Mitzvah) possibilities…This was confirmed on Saturday night when we established a synagogue Mitzvah Committee, complete with a preliminary list of initial programs to begin now rather than later, that all encompassing and often disappointing cover up term…With such a positive atmosphere, I made a suggestion I had made several times before, reminding the congregants that the project must be done with the utmost sense of respect: Sell one of the Torahs and use the money for Tzedakah.

It wasn't my idea. It came from the Talmud *(Megillah 27a)* and was later codified in the Shulchan Aruch *(Code of Jewish Law)*:

> *We may sell a synagogue, and similarly, all holy objects*
>
> *even a Sefer Torah in order to provide for students*
>
> *or to marry off orphans with the proceeds of the sale.*

(Orach Chaim 153:6)

Only Congregation Bnai Israel of Millburn, New Jersey, did something about it…the proceeds of their efforts went into a Tzedakah endowment fund.

Good People p. 209

Questions:

1. Why would you never want to sell a Sefer Torah? _____
_____

2. Under what circumstances may a congregation sell a Sefer Torah?
_____

3. How does this story demonstrate the concept of Covenant Community?
_____
_____

CLARA HAMMER: The Chicken Woman of Jerusalem

On a Friday morning in 1981, Clara Hammer, a resident of Jerusalem, was waiting in line at her local butcher shop to buy some chickens for her Shabbat meal. Shabbat, tradition tells us, is a time when we set our best table—the best dishes and silver, a crisp, clean tablecloth, candles, perhaps even fresh flowers—all to welcome the Sabbath Queen.

This particular Friday morning, Clara noticed her butcher handing a young girl a large plastic bag filled with chicken skin and bones—obviously it was not something anyone would feed their family. When it was finally Clara's turn to get her order, she asked the butcher, "How many cats and dogs does that young girl have? You gave her so much food for them."

Sadly, Mr. Hackar, Clara's butcher responded that what was in the bag was not for the youngster's pets, but rather, for her family. You see, the girl's father was very ill. Her mother did not work, and they didn't have enough money to buy food for Shabbat. Mr. Hackar also told Clara that he had given them food for a long time without asking for payment, but he could not continue doing that. So, with the leftovers he gave them, they were able to make soup, or, perhaps, some cholent (stew).

Horrified that anyone would have to eat such unhealthy food, Clara instructed the butcher to give the girl's family two chickens and a pound of ground turkey every Shabbat. She would pay the bill herself. She also insisted that they not know who was providing the food.

Soon, Clara heard about more families who did not have enough money to make a proper Shabbat and she decided to help them, as well. And, that is how Clara Hammer became known as "The Chicken Lady of Jerusalem" (if a family happens to be vegetarian, Clara will provide vegetarian fare as well) and that is how her charity fund began. People not only in Israel but all over the world have heard about her work and send her money to help pay for Shabbat meals. Sometimes, money comes from kids who share their Bar or Bat Mitzvah gifts or from a bride and groom who also want to share their simcha with others who are less fortunate. (Believe it or not, everyone who sends her money gets a personal thank you note written by Clara herself.) Today, even though Clara is what we might call "chronologically challenged," she continues her work. Since she started in 1981, hundreds and hundreds of families have enjoyed a sweeter Shabbat because she cared.

Questions on Clara Hammer:

1. Where does Clara live? _____

2. What was Clara doing at the butcher shop? _____

3. Why are Shabbat meals so important? _____

4. What was the butcher giving the young girl? Why? _____

5. Was the butcher "doing the right thing?" Why or why not?_____

6. Why was Clara upset? _____

7. What did she do about it? _____

8. How did Clara become the "Chicken Lady of Jerusalem?" _____

9. How does Clara's work relate to the concept of Kahal?_____

Things To Do

1. Do the exercise in *The New Jewish Experiential Book,* p. 207.
2. Work through the Torah Aura Instant Lesson entitled "Jewpiter 7" concerning a group of Jews colonizing a new planet.
3. Read Chapter Two, entitled, "Always Tag All Four Bases" of Joel Grishaver's book, *40 Things You Can Do To Save the Jewish People.*
4. What can we learn from Bnai Israel in Millburn? Do we all have too many "Torahs"—toys, shoes, jeans? How can we utilize the "more than we can use" to help others?
5. Count the Sifrei Torah in your synagogue. How many are used on a regular basis?
6. Ask someone familiar with the planning, implementing or raising of funds for Operation Moses (bringing Ethiopian Jews to Israel) or someone who traveled to the former Soviet Union to meet with Refuseniks to speak to the class. Ask them about their motives and, in the case of traveling to the former Soviet Union, their feelings while being there.
7. Invite the treasurer of the congregation into your class to discuss the problems congregations have when raising funds. Discuss what the funds are used for.
8. Take an inventory of the ritual objects in your congregation. Do you have a surplus of any item that can be sold for Tzedakah?

BASED UPON WHAT YOU HAVE LEARNED, WHAT WOULD DANNY DO?

_____

_____

_____

I: Our Story

A wealthy, pious man came before the Rabbi.

The Rabbi asked him, "Are you a devout person?"

"Oh Rabbi," he said, "I am so pious. During the week I eat only bread and thin soup. I fast whenever I can."

The Rabbi grew angry. "You are a wealthy man. You have a reputation in the community." He would not let the man go until he promised that he would eat meat every day.

The Rabbi's students were puzzled. "Why did you treat him like that?" they asked.

"Listen," said the Rabbi, "He is a wealthy man. If he lives on meat and wine every day, perhaps he will have pity on the poor and give them the money so that they can live on bread and thin soup. But if he lives on what the poor eat, he will expect them to live on stones."

Questions

1. How does the rich man think of himself? _____

_____

2. Is he right? Why or why not? _____

_____

3. Why is the Rabbi so upset at the rich man in this story? _____

_____

4. Do you think the Rabbi is right or wrong? Why? _____

_____

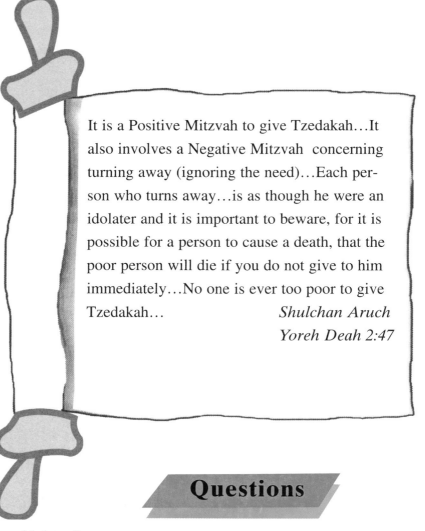

It is a Positive Mitzvah to give Tzedakah…It also involves a Negative Mitzvah concerning turning away (ignoring the need)…Each person who turns away…is as though he were an idolater and it is important to beware, for it is possible for a person to cause a death, that the poor person will die if you do not give to him immediately…No one is ever too poor to give Tzedakah…

Shulchan Aruch
Yoreh Deah 2:47

Questions

1. What is an idolator? _____

   _____

2. Why would a person who refuses to help poor people be called an idolator? _____

   _____

3. Why would a person who refuses to help poor people be violating the Brit? _____

   _____

4. How does a person who refuses to help poor people hurt the Kahal? _____

   _____

5. Why would that same person be guilty of murder? _____

   _____

6. What is this lesson's message concerning the importance of Tzedakah? _____

   _____

BARBARA BLOOM SILVERMAN: The Woman Who Likes to Cook

It was a hot, Friday afternoon in the Holy Land and Barbara Bloom Silverman was returning to her comfortable home with her husband at her side. When they passed an army checkpoint, Barbara could not help but notice the faces of the young soldiers, drenched with sweat from the hot sun and their heavy flak jackets. Here she was, returning to prepare for a Shabbat that would include a delicious meal and good friends and family who would grace her table. Barbara could not help but think of the difference in the way she and these brave soldiers were going to welcome the Sabbath bride. Why shouldn't they also enjoy a hot meal that was prepared at home with love and care?

That trip home was the beginning of Barbara Silverman's long career in feeding Israel's young soldiers. Barbara enlisted the aid of her husband and started cooking huge quantities of soup, chicken, kugels, dessert—whatever it would take to offer a delicious homemade Shabbat meal. They brought blankets to wrap around the soup pot, piled the remaining prepared foods into the car, and drove off to the checkpoint. Imagine the surprise on the faces of the soldiers when she showed up! A home cooked meal! Who would do such a thing? Barbara's cooking went on for months and eventually, the soldiers at this checkpoint pointed out that their friends at the checkpoint around the corner would also love this kind of a Shabbat meal. So—Barbara cooked even more. This special service continued until the Army decided that the area was too dangerous for Barbara and her husband to deliver the meals.

With the coming of the intifada in the fall of 2000, Barbara Silverman once again remembered the faces of the young soldiers and decided that she needed to do something to help. After all, she was again sitting in the comfort of home, while these young people were literally putting their lives on the line to make Israel safe. If she couldn't cook them a hot meal, why not send them a package filled with good, healthy snacks and other items that they could use like an extra pair of warm socks or a knitted cap to block the occasional cold winds of Israel's winters? And, so, A Package From Home was conceived. Barbara emailed all of her friends in the United States and in Israel and explained what she was doing. The checks started coming in. Soon, the newspapers heard about her work and publicized it.

More checks came. The Silverman home turned into an assembly line, when friends and volunteers appeared to help with the packing. During the summer, some of America's youth groups even joined in the effort! The soldiers receiving the packages also wrote. While the peanut butter and other healthy food was delicious, what they really wanted was some good junk food! Out went the peanut butter and into the packages went Israel's version of junk food—chips, that infamous Bamba, delicious brownies and cakes baked by a local baker. There is even a personal thank you note included in each box. With the help and cooperation of the army, Barbara continues to send thousands of packages to units placed on the front lines. Now, the army even sends a truck to pick the packages up.

As long as the funds are there, Barbara will continue to send these packages-made-with-love. After all, what better way is there to help those protecting our land?

Questions on Barbara Bloom Silverman

1. Where does Barbara live? _____

_____

2. What question did she ask when she saw the soldiers at the army check point? _____

_____

3. How did she start her project? _____

_____

4. How did Barbara's project expand? _____

_____

5. How does Barbara get support for her project? _____

_____

6. How does Barbara's project embody the concepts of Brit, Mitzvah and Kahal? _____

_____

7. What skills would someone need to do what Barbara does? _____

_____

54

STACEY WOLSTEN: Birthday Parties for All

There isn't a kid anywhere who doesn't look forward to his/her birthday. It is THEIR special day—they get to invite friends, eat lots of candy and ice cream, blow out the candles on a gooey chocolate cake and, maybe even play silly games like pin-the-tail-on-the-donkey or, if they are really lucky, take friends to the skating rink or to see the latest Arnold Schwarzenegger flick. Whatever they do, it is their day and to top it off they get lots of neat presents like their favorite PlayStation game or a new Barbie doll.

But what do you do if you and your family live in a homeless shelter? Or, perhaps, you have been moved to a safe house because there is violence in your family? How do you get your mail? How can friends come to visit? And if you are just a kid and your family doesn't have a lot of money, how do you celebrate your birthday? Not many people have thought about that. . . at least not until Stacey Wolsten came along.

You see, Stacey and her husband, Howard, wanted to get their kids involved in doing a Mitzvah project, something they could all do together. It was a great idea, but it wasn't so easy to arrange because most projects do not allow little kids to help. Fortunately, Stacey was a good "Mitzvah" thinker. She thought about those kids who have no place to call home-kids who must live in a shelter. How do they celebrate their birthday when they have none of their good friends living around them and their family doesn't have enough money to make a real party? And that is how the Happy Birthday Foundation started. The Wolstens approached a local shelter and asked if there was a child who was about to celebrate a birthday and when one was identified they went into action. They bought balloons, streamers, cake, ice cream, candy and of course, birthday gifts and took the party right to the shelter. Can you imagine the smiles that must have appeared on the birthday kid's face? And to top it off, Stacey and her family got so much joy and satisfaction themselves—just for remembering someone's birthday!

Today, hundreds of kids in New Jersey have been treated to a birthday party by the Happy Birthday Foundation. If the Wolsten family is doing this in New Jersey, why can't it be done in your hometown?

Questions

1. How did Stacey Wolstein get involved in her Mitzvah project? _____

_____

2. Why is the project so important? _____

_____

3. What steps could you take to do the same project in your community? _____

_____

BASED UPON WHAT YOU HAVE LEARNED, WHAT WOULD DANNY DO?

_____

_____

Vocabulary:

Lechem L'r'eyvim: Feeding the hungry.

לֶחֶם לִרְעֵבִים

There are two levels to every **Mitzvah**. The first level is the action necessary to perform the **Mitzvah**. The second level is the meaning behind the action. For example, look at this table of **Mitzvot**:

Mitzvah	Action	Meaning
Kiddush קִדּוּשׁ	Blessing the Wine	Remembering the Exodus from Egypt, remembering the Creation of the universe, blessing the day of Shabbat

How do we know this? Look at the text of the Kiddush for Shabbat.

Praised are You, Adonai our God, Sovereign of the universe
Creator of the fruit of the vine.
Praised are You, Lord our God, Sovereign of the universe,
Who has sanctified us through Your commandments,
Taking delight in us.
In love and favor You have given us the holy Shabbat
As a heritage,
In memory *of the work of creation.*
First of the holy days
In memory *of the liberation from Egypt.*
You chose us from among the peoples
In Your love and favor You made us holy
Giving us Your holy Shabbat as a joyous heritage.
Blessed are You, Adonai our God, who makes the Shabbat holy.

Now, let's look at the text of the Motzi:

Blessed are You, Adonai our God, Sovereign of the universe
Who brings forth bread from the earth.

Motzi	Blessing over bread	Blessing our ability to make food to keep us alive.
מוֹצִיא		Celebrating God's role in helping us make this food. Thanking God for this ability.

Fill in the Table of Mitzvot:

Mitzvah	Action	Meaning
Lighting Candles		
Kiddush		
Grace After Meals		
Hanukkah Lights		
Matza		
Purim Megillah		
Yom Kippur		

Our observance of Mitzvot is meant to bring joy and meaning into our lives. In this way, many of the Mitzvot we follow are meant to teach us meaningful lessons about life and community. They are meant to help us understand how to bring religious joy into our lives. One of the blessings said at the beginning of each holiday embodies this concept.

Blessed are You, Adonai our God, Sovereign of the universe,
Who has kept us alive / And established us,
Allowing us to reach this day.

Can you think of any special foods that are made during different holidays? Can you believe that there is a holiday where it is a Mitzvah to suffer? On Pesach we are commanded to relive our lives as slaves, eating poor bread (Matzah) and being hungry. On Yom Kippur we are commanded to "afflict our souls." The concept is called "ennui nefesh." The interpretation of this Mitzvah is that on Yom Kippur we are commanded to fast. Why would this be the Jewish definition of suffering? If the definition of suffering in Judaism is tied to the lack of food, then by providing food to those who need it, we are alleviating suffering in the world. What better way to achieve Tikun Olam?

One way to enter heaven is by feeding the hungry

(*Midrash Tehilim 118:17*)…

Nachum Ish Gamzu, one of Rabbi Akiva's teachers, narrated the following experience: I was once traveling to the house of my father-in-law, taking with me three donkeys – loads of food and drink. A starving man asked me for food. I answered that I would give him some when I unloaded, but before I could do so, he fell dead. I greatly grieved over his death, and prayed that the Lord send sufferings upon me in expiation for my sin. I should not have delayed my help, but should have cut through the load and given him food at once   (*Taanit, 21*)…

Advice and words will not fill an empty belly

(*Mishle Yehoshua*)

One way: Are there other ways to enter heaven? What does it mean to "enter heaven"? How does one "feed the hungry"? Is it enough to feed just one person?

Ish Gamzu: "Gamzu" in Hebrew means "This too." Nachum was called "Ish Gamzu" because he was a man (ish) who always said, no matter what happened, "This too (gamzu) is for the good." No matter how bad things seemed, he could find something positive to talk about.

Rabbi Akiva: He was the most important rabbi of his time.

Food and drink: Why would anyone travel with a lot of food and drink to the home of a relative? Why was Nachum going there?

When I unloaded: If his donkeys were loaded with food and drink, couldn't he just reach into a sack and pull out something to eat for the man? What type of food did he intend to give the starving man?

I greatly grieved: Why did he grieve? What had Nachum done wrong? Was it his fault that the man was starving?

Upon me: Did Nachum deserve to be punished for what he did? Why?

Advice and words: What kind of advice and words would a poor person most likely hear when they ask for food?

One way to enter heaven is by feeding the hungry

(Midrash Tehilim 118:17)...

Nachum Ish Gamzu, one of Rabbi Akiva's teachers, narrated the following experience: I was once traveling to the house of my father-in-law, taking with me three donkeys – loads of food and drink. A starving man asked me for food. I answered that I would give him some when I unloaded, but before I could do so, he fell dead. I greatly grieved over his death, and prayed that the Lord send sufferings upon me in expiation for my sin. I should not have delayed my help, but should have cut through the load and given him food at once

(Taanit, 21)...

Advice and words will not fill an empty belly *(Mishle Yehoshua)*

One way: _____

_____

Ish Gamzu: _____

_____

_____

Rabbi Akiva:. _____

Food and drink: _____

_____

When I unloaded: _____

_____

_____

I greatly grieved: _____

_____

Upon me: _____

_____

Advice and words: _____

_____

Cohen-Hillel Academy (of Marblehead, Mass.) donates leftover food both from its hot lunch program and also from the lunches the children bring to school.

My friend Marilyn Moses is in charge of the hot lunch program. The following is part of a letter she sent me reviewing the school's program:

I am able to encourage volunteers to help us serve food twice a week. During the time we work together, I am able to recognize when someone is in need. All our volunteers are invited to take home "goody bags." In order to respect their Kavod (dignity), I let them know that they will be able to save time later in the day and not have to worry about what to prepare for dinner for their family...

Whenever I see anyone—student, volunteer or staff person without a lunch for any reason, I make sure they enjoy one of our lunches...

*A number of our 7th grade students are organizing a **Mitzvah** or **Tzedakah** project with leftover food— both items they bring from home and items left over from our lunch program...These children have contacted Jewish Family Services and other agencies in the area. The children arrange with agreeable adults how to transport these donations. One of the agencies in our area is a soup kitchen called **"My Brother's Table."** There are also shelters...*

Good People, p. 123

Questions:

1. How does the Cohen Hillel Academy perform the Mitzvah of Lechem L'r'eyvim? _____
_____

2. Where do they get the food from? _____
_____

3. Why are the "volunteers" encouraged to take home "goody bags?" _____
_____

4. What reasons are given for taking the food home? _____
_____

5. Why is it done this way? _____
_____

6. How do the children arrange to perform the Mitzvah of Lechem L'r'eyvim?_____
_____

SYD MANDELBAUM: Rock 'n' Rollin'

Have you ever wondered what goes on backstage at a rock concert? How many days before a concert does the group spend rehearsing? What do they eat during those rehearsals? Are they limited to a few cans of soda and some bags of chips? What do they eat after the long, hard performance has ended? For the big event, do they call in for a pizza? Burgers?

Well, they certainly do spend long hours rehearsing and they do eat a lot. Playing in a rock band under the hot lights really works up your appetite. They don't, however, limit their diet to burgers, fries and shakes. Backstage, both before and after concerts, is like a royal banquet. We're talking major food here, and lots of it.

Enter, Syd Mandelbaum. After visiting a local dinner theater several years ago he asked a friend (who happened to be a rock promoter) what was done with the leftovers. "Garbage," his friend replied, "they just go into the dumpster." From there it was easy. With a little bit of "mitzvah thinking," Syd deduced that what was available at this one theater must be available at theaters all over the country. That was an awful lot of food and it was probably all being tossed into the garbage. A lot of hungry people could be fed with that food and with that idea came Syd's project, Rock and Wrap It Up!

Syd has made contact with more than a hundred rock bands, most with very familiar names like Santana, Aerosmith or Hootie and the Blowfish. By adding a simple line to their contracts, bands are assuring the retrieval of tons of food from concerts all over the country. By recruiting volunteers throughout the States (as well as some cities in Europe), Syd knows that the leftovers will go from the backstage party to the local food pantry with a minimum of trouble and waste.

Imagine the faces on people eating at a local shelter when a platter of fresh turkey or sliced steak is placed before them. That's frequently the kind of food that gets picked up from these concerts.

Why stop at a rock concert? What happens to the food that is served during the shooting of a movie? Where do the leftovers go on election night, when politicians all over the country gather at parties to celebrate (or cry) with hundreds of friends and supporters? And the big question for school kids is where do the leftovers from the school cafeteria go?

Syd Mandelbaum has come up with a solution to each of these situations. It wasn't really difficult. We all know places that serve tons of food and then throw out the leftovers. Why can't those leftovers go to hungry people?

QUESTIONS ON SYD MANDELBAUM:

1. What kind of food is served backstage at rock concerts? Why? _____

_____

2. Who is Syd Mandelbaum? _____

_____

3. What "question" did he ask?   _____

_____

4. Why did Syd get in touch with rock bands? _____

_____

5. Did the rock bands respond? _____

_____

6. How hard is it to get a response from a rock star? _____

_____

7. What kind of "questions" could you ask? _____

_____

8. What special talents did Syd have to make "Rock and Wrap It Up!" successful? _____

_____

9. What other places can you think of that serve large amounts of food that could be retrieved and served to hungry people? _____

_____

Things To Do

1. Start a canned food collection drive in your congregation/school. Place a food basket in the entrance of your congregation/school so that people can donate at all times.

2. Around Thanksgiving or Pesach, have a special food drive.

3. Find out where the leftovers from your congregation go. If the answer is "in the garbage," do not accept that. Call Ziv or another agency for help.

4. Volunteer to work as a class for a shelter or soup kitchen. Feed hungry people!

5. Brainstorm ways to help feed the poor. For example,
   a. Give up a weekly candy bar or pack of sports cards.
   b. Clip coupons from the paper.
   c. Create a school bulletin board displaying ideas.
   d. Hold a contest for the most creative idea.

6. Go "dumpster dipping." Don't forget your rubber gloves. Take a tour of the garbage bins behind stores in your area. See how much food is being thrown away.

7. Try Nachum Ish Gamzu for his alleged crime of delayed Tzedakah. Assign members of your class as defendant, prosecutors, defense attorney, judges and jury. Is he guilty? Is so, of what?

Focus on One Activity: Start a Canned Food Drive

Ask the following questions:

1. Are there hungry people in our community?_____

   _____

2. How can we find out about them?_____

   _____

3. What organizations are there that help feed the hungry?_____

   _____

4. What can we do to help?_____

   _____

Actions to be Taken

1. Ask your congregation's social action committee if your class can lead a canned food drive for the congregation.

2. Contact local food distribution centers to see how you will get the food to them.

3. Choose a date (at least 6 weeks away) for the canned food drive.

4. Write an article for the congregation bulletin about the food drive.

5. Send out a mailing to the congregation about the food drive.

6. Find a place to store the food that is donated.

7. Get some boxes and put the food into them.

8. Get volunteers to collect the food being dropped off on that day.

9. Arrange for the food to be picked up by a social service agency.

BASED UPON WHAT YOU HAVE LEARNED, WHAT WOULD DANNY DO?

_____

_____

_____

_____

_____

Take a moment and draw a picture or write a paragraph depicting an example of Tzedakah.

Vocabulary:

Tzedakah: Justice, doing the right thing.
צְדָקָה

Hachnasat Orchim: Welcoming the stranger.
הַכְנָסַת אוֹרְחִים

    Over the last several lessons we have learned that **Tzedakah** is a Mitzvah: one of many that bind us together in a **Covenant** Community. We have learned that **Tzedakah** is something required of us. However, if we were to ask anyone what the definition of **Tzedakah** was, they would say, "charity," or "giving money to the poor."

    In a sense they would be right. After all, what classroom doesn't have a **Tzedakah** box? How many times does the rabbi or your teacher talk about "giving **Tzedakah?**"

    But that is not what **Tzedakah** is. **Tzedakah** means "justice," or "the right thing." When we talk about giving or doing **Tzedakah** we are talking about "doing the right thing." There are many ways of doing the right thing, and many things that can be done right. The use of money to help needy people is only one example. There are many others.

In the next several lessons we will learn about several **Mitzvot** that are important for our community and can also teach us something about helping those in need. The first **Mitzvah** is called **Hachnasat Orchim** (welcoming guests).

In the Torah, the most wicked place of all was the city of Sodom. A legend tells us how every person in need and asking for money would be given gold pieces by the residents of Sodom. Each piece would have the name of the person who gave it on one side. The stranger would be overwhelmed by the generosity of the Sodomites, giving him gold when all he needed was money for bread. However, no one would sell him any food. After he starved to death, the Sodomites would find the body and take back their gold coins.

The unfriendly atmosphere of Sodom is described by how they would mistreat strangers. We learn that evil people are those who deny others shelter and food. While there are many stories about how wicked the inhabitants of Sodom were, it is the stories about how they mistreated strangers that tell us how hateful they were.

The idea of **Hachnasat Orchim** is very important to our community. Jews have been wandering for many centuries. Without our ability to find comfort and shelter with other Jews around the world, many would have suffered throughout our history.

Questions on Beauty and the Beast

Film: Beauty and the Beast (0:00:00–0:02:30)

1. What type of person is the prince? _____
_____

2. Who knocks on the prince's door? _____
_____

3. What does she ask? _____
_____

4. What does the prince answer? _____
_____

5. What does she offer the prince? _____
_____

6. Why does the prince reject her? _____
_____

7. What is the prince's punishment? _____
_____

8. What must the beast do in order to overcome the punishment? _____
_____

9. Do you think there is a connection between having love in one's heart and hospitality?
_____
_____

God appeared to him (Abraham) at Elonay Mamray. He (Abraham) was sitting at the opening of the tent during the heat of the day. He lifted his eyes to see and there were three men standing over him. **He ran** from the opening of the tent to **greet them** and he (Abraham) bowed to the ground. He said, **"My lords, if I have found favor** in your eyes do not pass before me. Take a little water and **wash your feet.** Rest here under the tree. I will take a slice of bread and you will refresh yourselves. Then you can go... *(Genesis 18:1-5)*...

When a stranger came to the city of **S'dom** and asked for hospitality, the residents of S'dom did not refuse him but forced the stranger to sleep in a bed provided by them. If the bed were too small for him, they would cut off his legs until his body fitted the bed. If the bed was too large, they would stretch his head and feet, so that even though he lost his life, **his body was made to fit** *(conform)*... *(Sanhedrin 109b)*

Hospitality is even more important than encountering **God's intimate presence** *(Shabbat 127a)*

God appeared: We know that God appeared to Abraham. The text tells us that Abraham saw three strangers. Is this important?

He ran: Why did Abraham run to greet the strangers?

Greet them: Notice that Abraham performed three different actions; he ran, he greeted them and he bowed to the ground. Why were all three necessary? What purpose did each of the actions serve?

My lords: This is a term of respect. Why did Abraham speak in such a manner to the strangers? He didn't know who they were. Why is this title of respect important to the performance of the Mitzvah of Hachnasat Orchim?

If I have found favor: Why does Abraham speak to them in this way? Why does he tell them that they will be doing him a favor if they accept his hospitality?

Wash your feet: Why is washing your feet the first thing they would want to do? Why is it so important to the performance of this Mitzvah?

S'dom: This city was known as a very evil place.

His body was made to fit: How did the residents of S'dom make Hachnasat Orchim evil? Is it possible to abuse this Mitzvah? If so, how?

God's intimate presence: Why would performing Hachnasat Orchim be more important than being close to God?

Texts on Hachnasat Orchim: Hospitality

God appeared to him (Abraham) at Elonay Mamray. He (Abraham) was sitting at the opening of the tent during the heat of the day. He lifted his eyes to see and there were three men standing over him. **He ran** from the opening of the tent to **greet them** and he (Abraham) bowed to the ground. He said, **"My lords, if I have found favor** in your eyes do not pass before me. Take a little water and **wash your feet.** Rest here under the tree. I will take a slice of bread and you will refresh yourselves. Then you can go…   *(Genesis 18:1-5)…*

When a stranger came to the city of **S'dom** and asked for hospitality, the residents of S'dom did not refuse him but forced the stranger to sleep in a bed provided by them. If the bed were too small for him, they would cut off his legs until his body fitted the bed. If the bed was too large, they would stretch his head and feet, so that even though he lost his life, **his body was made to fit** *(conform)…*   *(Sanhedrin 109b)*

Hospitality is even more important than encountering **God's intimate presence**   *(Shabbat 127a)*

God appeared: _____

_____

He ran: _____
Greet them: _____

_____

_____

My lords: _____

_____

_____

If I have found favor: _____

_____

Wash your feet: _____

_____

S'dom: _____
His body was made to fit: _____

_____

God's intimate presence: _____

_____

CARIDAD ASENSIO

In 1960, when Caridad Asensio was a young girl in Cuba, a revolution put a new government in control of the country. The Asensio family fled to the United States, starting life over in Florida. It's not easy to emigrate from your homeland to a new place. But as she grew up, Caridad could see that there were people for whom life was even more difficult than for the Cuban refugees: the migrant workers on Florida's farms.

Most farms need a large work force for just a few weeks a year, when the crops are harvested. The people who do the harvesting are "migrants," moving from farm to farm as they are needed. They have no permanent homes because they are always on the move. They are paid very little and have no health care, no paid vacations, none of the benefits that other working people take for granted. Children in migrant families are in and out of school because they're always on the move. Even when they are in one place for a while, many of them work in the fields with their families instead of going to school.

Caridad Asensio saw all this and didn't like it at all. She thought that no one should have to endure such a difficult life. She put her concern into action. Caridad started the Migrant Association of South Florida—an organization that helps migrants become full time members of communities. She finds stable jobs for them, so they do not have to go "where the work is." She buys trailers and gives them to migrant families so they can move in and settle down. Her beautiful clinic offers comprehensive medical care with the help of 200 doctors and nurses who volunteer their services. The families who escape the migrant life have new hope. They can raise their children in stable communities, thanks to Caridad and her devoted staff

Questions on Caridad Asensio

1. Where was Caridad born? _____

2. Why was Caridad's family forced to flee their country? _____

3. What did Caridad learn from this experience? _____

4. Who are the people Caridad helps? _____

5. What are some of the problems they face? _____

6. How does Caridad solve their problems? _____

7. How does Caridad embody the Mitzvah of "Hachnasat Orchim?" _____

Thoughts from Danny Siegel

Through our connections with the inspiring Caridad Asensio, we have purchased a mobile home ($2,300) to be used as a permanent home for a family of five migrant workers. Caridad is a most extraordinary woman. The remaining $1,000 went to her medical clinic and other pressing needs of the people she reaches in the South Florida area.

A Washington Jewish organization involved with decent housing for everyone sponsors a program of home repair whereby crews go out and, often in one day, complete a thorough fix-up.

Good People, pp. 93-94

Questions

1. What is a migrant worker? Where are they found? _____

   _____

2. What is a mobile home? _____

   _____

3. How big is a mobile home? How many people can live in it? _____

   _____

4. What type of family would be happy to have a mobile home as a permanent home? Why? _____

   _____

5. Why would a family living in this mobile home need to have a medical clinic? _____

   _____

6. What other "pressing needs" would this family have? _____

   _____

Hachnasat Orchim: Things To Do

1. Are there any organizations like Habitat for Humanity in your area? Look for organizations that create or renovate housing for the homeless. Look through the Yellow Pages or on the internet for organizations in your area.

2. Does your congregation make provisions for finding Seders or holiday meals for students or people living alone? If not, try to organize a program for Passover or Rosh Hashanah or any other upcoming holiday (including Shabbat).

3. Does your congregation have a Shabbat exchange program where different family units invite newer members to their homes for a Shabbat dinner?

4. Is there an organization in your area that provides shelter for the homeless on a weekly basis? If so, would your congregation be willing to house "guests" for a week (perhaps between Christmas and New Years?)

5. Discuss how Hachnasat Orchim could be practiced in school? During the day?

HACHNASAT ORCHIM: Focus on One Activity

Shabbat Exchange Program:

1. Appoint two members of the class to approach the membership committee to ask their permission to plan this program.

2. Get a list of new members from the congregation office (a new member is someone who has joined within the last year).

3. Get a list of board members from the congregation office.

4. Send a letter (similar to this one) to each of the board members:

Dear _____,

> *As members of the _____ grade, we have asked the membership committee for permission to start a "Shabbat Exchange" program. In this program, veteran members of the congregation invite new members to their homes for a Shabbat meal. It is a good way for people to get to know one another, make new friends and fulfill the mitzvah of "Hachnasat Orchim," hospitality. As a member of the board, we would like to ask you if you would volunteer to be the "veteran member" for the Shabbat exchange program. Please let us know as soon as possible so that we can plan the program.*
>
>

Sincerely,

Members of the _____ grade.

5. Send the following letter to all new members:

Dear _____,

> *As members of the _____ grade in Congregation _____, we would like to welcome you to our community. We are trying to start a "Shabbat Exchange" program, where veteran members of the congregation perform the Mitzvah of "Hachnasat Orchim," hospitality, by hosting new members of the congregation to a Shabbat dinner.*
>
> *We would like to ask you to be a "new member" to be hosted by a veteran member. Please let us know as soon as possible if you would like to take part so that we can arrange the program.*
>
>

Sincerely,

The _____ grade.

6. When you get the responses, match a "veteran member" with a "new member." Have the veteran member contact the new member to invite him/her to Shabbat dinner.

7. If you can, find out when the two member units will be together, and send a special card to both families, thanking them for participating in the program.

BASED UPON WHAT YOU HAVE LEARNED, WHAT WOULD DANNY DO?

_____

_____

_____

_____

_____

_____

_____

_____

_____

_____

Vocabulary:

Bikkur Cholim: Visiting people who are sick.
בִּקּוּר חוֹלִים

Most people don't know that there are many ways of performing the Mitzvah of **Tzedakah**. There are many ways of "doing the right thing." In the last lesson we learned about the **Mitzvah** of **Hachnasat Orchim**, hospitality.

Is it possible to perform the **Mitzvah** of **Hachnasat Orchim** outside the home? The Mitzvah is about being a host. In order to be a good host it is important to be friendly, warm, and most of all, caring and considerate of others.

Tzedakah teaches us that we must provide support for those in need. Of all the people you will ever know, people who are ill top the list of those in need. There are different types of poverty. A person can be poor if they have little money or a person can be poor if they have poor health. No matter what else, caring for the poor makes a person special.

If you ask someone who has been a patient in a hospital, or if you yourself have been a patient in a hospital, you will learn that it can be a very lonely and scary experience. People are not comfortable in hospitals. Think what happens there.

- You usually only go there when you are sick.
- Many people suffer pain while there.
- You wear funny outfits that don't cover your whole body.
- Many people undergo unpleasant medical procedures.
- You see those you love most when they have the least control of their surroundings.
- The food is lousy.
- Little children are not allowed to visit.
- You can't see your pets there.
- No one looks happy there.

If we truly care about someone, we want to see them get well and are genuinely concerned for their welfare. Also, as member of a Covenant Community we are responsible for one another and that most especially includes people who are ill, as well as people who are healthy.

One big difference between **Bikkur Cholim** and other **Mitzvot** is that you have to go somewhere, perhaps far away, to perform this **Mitzvah**. Most other **Mitzvot** are performed at home, in the congregation or in school. **Bikkur Cholim** also requires you to approach someone else and do something for them to perform the **Mitzvah**. Most important of all, **Bikkur Cholim** is a **Mitzvah** that cannot be done improperly.

When we read the verse "Blessed is he who considers the poor." (Psalms 41:1) Rav Huna said, **"That is** he who visits the sick." (Vayikra Rabba, Behar 34:1)... Rabbi Akiva said, "He who does not visit the sick is as if he shed blood."

(Nedarim 40a)...

There is no limit as regards the visitation of the sick. What does this mean? **Rav Yosef** argued that it meant that there is no limit to its reward. Abaye said to him, "Is there a limit to the reward of any of the Mitzvot?"...**Abaye** continued, "The phrase 'no limit' means that (even) the great (people) must visit the small (insignificant) people." It once happened that one of **Rabbi Akiva's** students became ill, and none of the sages visited him. Then Rabbi Akiva himself went to the disciple's house, and because he saw to it that the floor was swept and sprinkled with water, the man recovered. "My master, you have restored me to life," the student said. **Akiva went out and taught,** "One who does not visit the sick is like someone who sheds blood."

(Nedarim 39b – 40a)...

A visitor came to see a sick man and asked what ailed him. After the sick man told him, the visitor said: "Oh, my father died of the same disease." The sick man became very upset, but the visitor said, "Don't worry, I'll pray to God to heal you." To which the sick man answered: "And when you pray, add that I may be spared visits from any more **foolish people.**"

That is: Why is a sick person considered like a poor person? Why would a person who visits a sick person be blessed?

Rav Yosef: What is the disagreement between Rav Yosef and Rav Huna? Is Rav Huna suggesting that visiting the sick is the most important of any of the Mitzvot? Why or why not?

Abaye: Does Abaye agree with Rav Huna? How does Abaye interpret the phrase "no limit?"

Rabbi Akiva: Was the leading rabbi of his generation. Why would people not visit a sick person? What did Akiva do for his student? How does the story of Rabbi Akiva and his student illustrate Abaye's teaching?

Akiva taught: Why is not visiting a sick person like shedding blood?

Foolish person: Why was this visitor foolish?

When we read the verse "Blessed is he who considers the poor." (Psalms 41:1) Rav Huna said, **"That is** he who visits the sick." (Vayikra Rabba, Behar 34:1)… Rabbi Akiva said, "He who does not visit the sick is as if he shed blood."

(Nedarim 40a)…

There is no limit as regards the visitation of the sick. What does this mean? **Rav Yosef** argued that it meant that there is no limit to its reward. Abaye said to him, "Is there a limit to the reward of any of the Mitzvot?"…**Abaye** continued, "The phrase 'no limit' means that (even) the great (people) must visit the small (insignificant) people." It once happened that one of **Rabbi Akiva's** students became ill, and none of the sages visited him. Then Rabbi Akiva himself went to the disciple's house, and because he saw to it that the floor was swept and sprinkled with water, the man recovered. "My master, you have restored me to life," the student said. **Akiva went out and taught,** "One who does not visit the sick is like someone who sheds blood." *(Nedarim 39b – 40a)…*

A visitor came to see a sick man and asked what ailed him. After the sick man told him, the visitor said: "Oh, my father died of the same disease." The sick man became very upset, but the visitor said, "Don't worry, I'll pray to God to heal you." To which the sick man answered: "And when you pray, add that I may be spared visits from any more **foolish people."**

That is: _____

_____

Rav Yosef: _____

_____

Abaye: _____

Rabbi Akiva: _____

_____

Akiva taught: _____

Foolish person: _____

The Problem: Unhappy kids, sad kids, kids whose hair has fallen out because of cancer therapy. Unhappy adults, sad adults, adults whose hair has fallen out because of cancer therapy, all kinds of other sad and unhappy people in hospitals and institutions.

Solution #1: Learn clowning, dress up as a clown, and go into the hospitals and institutions and make people happy.

Solved by: Many, many clowns.

Solution #2: Teach clowning in the religious school. Have the graduates go into hospitals and institutions and make people happy.

Solved by: Sweet Pea and Buttercup, also known as Mike and Sue Turk, Millburn, New Jersey.

Good People, p. 115

Questions

1. What do you know about cancer? _____

_____

2. How must it feel to be very sick? _____

_____

3. How important is your hair? Why? _____

_____

4. What makes a clown funny? _____

_____

5. Why would a clown make a kid with cancer feel better? _____

_____

7. How does a clown fulfill the Mitzvah of Bikkur Cholim? _____

_____

MIKE AND SUE TURK: *Just Clowning Around*

If you were to meet Mike and Sue Turk on the street, you would comment, "what a good looking, wonderful couple they are!" You would be seeing only one side of them. The truth is, Mike and Sue lead a double life. In their spare time, they take on completely different personalities—they even look different, and. . . they have different names.

Sometimes, Mike and Sue become Buttercup and Sweetpea. They might have blue hair, a large red nose, floppy ears and feet and wear the most outrageous clothes. Buttercup even sports a flower in his lapel that will squirt water in your face if he decides to make you laugh! Sweetpea and Buttercup are Mitzvah clowns and, as Mitzvah clowns, their job is to bring laughter and cheer to anyone who might be sick or lonely or just plain sad.

On any given day, you might find them in a local hospital visiting children who are seriously ill. Children attached to tubes and machines, children with little or no hair on their head because of the drugs they have been given to get rid of the cancer in their body. All benefit from their visit. They might receive a clown button or even a balloon twisted into the shape of a giraffe. They will always end up laughing and smiling, forgetting the pain and sadness of their illness.

On another day, you might find them in a nursing home making the elderly residents laugh with their pratfalls and jokes. If any of the residents want to dance the way they used to, Buttercup will gladly take their hand and do a waltz or even a hora! Even elderly people need cheering up. It can be very lonely without your familiar possessions or family around you, and a clown can chase that loneliness away, even if it is only for a short time.

And, on even another day you might find

Buttercup and Sweetpea teaching children or adults how they, too, can be Mitzvah clowns. In their classes, you can learn to use your own talents for the wonderful art of clowning.

WARNING! Clowning doesn't make just those whom you visit feel good. If you learn to become a clown you, too, will get a good feeling. That's what happens when you help others.

I: Our Story

Once, on a bitter cold night, as Rabbi Yosef was teaching his students, he heard a knock on his door: It was Baruch. Baruch was a very poor laborer with a wife and new child at home. He looked desperate.

"Rabbi Yosef, I haven't earned much these last weeks. We don't have enough money to heat our home. It is so cold and I am afraid that my wife and baby will suffer. What can I do?"

Rabbi Yosef gave him what he had, sent him to buy some coal, and told him he would be out to see him later that night. After Baruch left, his students asked him what he intended to do. "I am going to see Reb Nissen," was his reply. Reb Nissin was the wealthiest man in the town – but also the most miserly. No one had ever been able to get him to give to anyone or anything.

Rabbi Yosef went up to his door, with his students watching from afar. He knocked on Reb Nissin's door. The servant answered and asked what his business was. Rabbi Yosef told him he wanted to see Reb Nissin. The servant invited him in to wait but Rabbi Yosef answered that he would wait outside.

Stamping his feet to keep warm, Rabbi Yosef waited a few minutes. Reb Nissin opened the door and exclaimed, "Rabbi Yosef, what are you waiting out here for? Come in and warm yourself. Then we can talk."

Rabbi Yosef replied, "No thank you. I don't want to be a bother. I just have a simple question to ask."

Reb Nissin, shivering in the cold, pleaded with him, "There is no need to be so uncomfortable." But Rabbi Yosef again said, "I don't want to be a bother." He continued, "There is a poor man who lives not far from here who needs money to heat his home. Do you think you could help him out?"

Reb Nissin dug deeply into his pockets and came up with a very generous sum. He told Rabbi Yosef, "Please take this to him. Tell him to come around tomorrow if he needs some work. I will see what I can do."

His students were amazed. "Rabbi Yosef" they cried, "How did you do it? How did you get Reb Nissin to contribute?"

What do you think Rabbi Yosef answered? _____

_____

_____

Text on Who is Responsible to Give? Who is Fitting to Receive?

Everyone is required to give Tzedakah. Even one who is poor and is supported by Tzedakah is required to give from what he receives. One who gives less than it is acceptable the courts can punish him with blows as a rebellious person until he gives, and his assets may be taxed in front of him as they take from him what is appropriate to give…Orphans are not required to give Tzedakah even for ransoming the captives, even if they have sufficient funds…A man who gives more money than he can afford or if he gives too much in order not to be embarrassed…The Gabbai is not allowed to take Tzedakah from him…

Yoreh Deah: 248

1. Why would a poor person be required to give Tzedakah? _____

_____

2. From this text, who is considered a rebellious person? _____

_____

3. Why are they considered a rebellious person? _____

_____

4. Do you think the courts should have the right to force people to give Tzedakah?

   Why or why not? _____

_____

5. Why would the Gabbai be ordered not to take Tzedakah from someone who gives

   too much? _____

_____

6. Why are orphans not required to give Tzedakah? _____

_____

When you look at her, you would never guess her story. She is short, petite and speaks with a distinctive accent, definitely Israeli, but with a hint of her German past. You know immediately that she is filled with energy and spirit. When you hear her story—it all comes into place. Trudi Birger is a child of the Holocaust. In 1933 she was a young girl living in Frankfurt, Germany, with her parents and brother. Trudi's was a life of privilege and culture. Her father was a manufacturer and Trudi and her brother lived in a fine home, filled with beautiful furniture and much love. All of that security and happiness came crashing down in 1933 when the German army marched into town. First Trudi and her mother and brother witnessed the loss of their husband and father, and eventually other family members disappeared as well. At one point, Trudi's brother was separated from them. They had no idea of the horrors that may have befallen him. Trudi and her mother worked as forced laborers in many different places and eventually ended up in the concentration camps. It was only through sheer luck and Trudi's incredible cunning and bravery that both of them survived and eventually made their way to Palestine. (At this point, they were reunited with her brother, who also survived the camps.)

When you learn about Trudi's earliest years, somehow it all comes together. It is then that you can make sense of everything that she has accomplished as an individual in her new home, Israel. Trudi's first effort was to establish a program in Jerusalem called Dental Volunteers for Israel. As she witnessed, first-hand, the poor dental hygiene practiced by the city's very poorest citizens, she knew that something had to be done. In places like the United States, even poor children who are enrolled in public school get some dental care. In Israel, that is not the case and to make matters worse, Israeli children eat a large amount of sugar which, along with poor dental hygiene, is a formula for disaster—serious dental disease, pain, and eventual loss of teeth. Dental Volunteers for Israel, DVI, provides complete dental care for many poor children. The clinic is staffed by volunteer dentists who come to work from countries around the world. If you are willing to give two weeks of your time and buy a plane ticket, Trudi will do all of the rest. You will have use of a furnished apartment and even get an occasional pass to a cultural event or swimming at one of Jerusalem's beautiful hotels. It is Trudi who is the driving force behind this project. She is the one who begs and prods to gather not only funds for ongoing expenses, but also critical dental equipment and supplies.

You would certainly think that this program, alone, would take up most of Trudi's time and energy, but you would be wrong. Trudi is devoted to one other cause—her families in the Romema neighborhood of Jerusalem. If you know the city, you know that Romema is one of the poorest parts of Jerusalem. The children who live here rarely escape this poverty. That is, unless they are part of Trudi's work.

Trudi knows that education is the key to breaking the cycle of poverty and works tirelessly to change the dynamic. She works with many families, giving them school supplies (a very expensive necessity in Israel), providing funds for food, housing and other basics. She continually encourages the children and their parents, reminding them of the importance of a good education. Today, Trudi can proudly point to many, many children who did break that cycle of poverty and are now independent, hard working citizens of the State of Israel.

Questions on Trudi Birger

1. How did Trudi grow up? _____
_____

2. How did her experiences as a child influence her work in Israel? _____
_____

3. What organization did Trudi found in Israel? Why? _____
_____

4. In what other ways has she tried to help people? _____
_____

5. What makes Trudi a hero? _____
_____

When was the last time you ate? Did you have any trouble getting what you wanted to eat? Have you ever had to forgo a candy bar or ice cream cone because you didn't have enough money to buy it? When was the last time you went without something to eat because the kitchen shelves were bare? This is a scene that is repeated over and over again throughout our country.

The statistics are sobering: 29% of children under the age of 12 in this country are hungry or at risk of hunger. In 1995, statistics showed that almost 12 million households in this country faced hunger or food insecurity at least once a month. This represented more than 34 million people. A 1997 study showed that more than 27% of all food produced for human consumption in this country is wasted each year. In real numbers? Almost 96 billion pounds of food, 365 pounds for every man, woman and child in this country. In 1997, requests for emergency food assistance rose 16%.

What is the root cause of hunger? The statistics cited prove that it is a *not* because there is shortage of food. We grow enough food to feed all the hungry people in the world. The root cause of hunger is our inability to deliver the food to the places where people are hungry. Thus millions of pounds of fresh fruit and vegetables rot and are wasted before they can feed hungry people.

Did you know that millions of pounds of vegetables and fruit are thrown out every year because they might be bruised? We don't want to eat an apple with tiny spots or a potato that has too many bumps. It

doesn't look good. This food is usually thrown out, because there is no way to deliver it to people who are hungry.

To Ken Horne and Ray Buchanan the problem of how to get that food to where it is needed was solved by their program, The Potato Project. The Project delivers about fifteen million pounds of produce to hungry people every year. The food is generally donated by growers, shippers, brokers and processors. The Potato Project then pays for packaging and shipping the food to agencies that will distribute it. The total cost? About two cents per serving. That's a pretty good return on your investment.

In addition to moving all of those fruits and vegetables, Ken and Ray started the Seed Potato Project. This program provides seed potatoes to communities all over our country so that needy families can plant and harvest their own crops. In rural America, where land is plentiful, what better way to get food to hungry people than to make it possible for them grow their own.

When it comes to Mitzvah thinking to solve the hunger problem in this country the possibilities are limitless. Ken Horne, Ray Buchanan and The Potato Project have proven that.

BASED UPON WHAT YOU HAVE LEARNED, WHAT WOULD DANNY DO?

13 HEDUR PNAI ZAKEN: Respect for Elders

Vocabulary:

Hedur Pnai Zaken: Respect for Elders

הִדוּר פְּנֵי זָקֵן

If you made a list of the elderly people you know very well, who would be on it? How old is old? Is your teacher an elderly person? Is anyone over 21 years old? How well do you know them? Do you have any friends who are old?

What makes old people happy? What makes them sad? What makes old people afraid? What are their lives like?

Chances are that you know about old people from being with your grandparents or other relatives their age and through TV programs and movies. Is there a difference between how your older relatives act and how old people are shown in the movies?

It would be unusual if you really did know the answer to all these questions. In our society, elderly people are usually not encouraged to share their feelings about themselves with younger people. Often they tend to stay "with their own kind" and have little interaction with children.

In general, old people (grandparents and relatives) know more about you than you know about them. This is sad because old people are "people." They have fears, hopes and joys just like everyone else. We tend to treat elderly people as frail and delicate children. We do not treat them as adult human beings in frail circumstances. We do not see them as people who are in command of most of their faculties, just unable to do for themselves what was once possible.

As a Covenant community, we have a responsibility to care for those who cannot care for themselves. We have a responsibility to appreciate the past contributions of members who may be "broken" in body and spirit.

Respecting the aged of any community is a very important Mitzvah. In some ways, a community is judged by how it treats those whose bodies have begun to betray them. But, what does it mean to respect? How does one "respect" an elder?

One answer is given in the Jerusalem Talmud:

A man may feed his father fattened chickens and inherit Gehenna (hell).
Another may put his father to work treading a mill and inherit the Garden of Eden (heaven).
How is it possible for a man to feed his father fattened chickens and still inherit Gehenna?
There was a man who used to feed his father fattened chickens.
Once his father asked him, "My son, where did you get these?"
He answered, "Old man, old man, shut up and eat just as the dogs shut up when they eat."
Such a man inherits Gehenna.
How is it possible for a man to put his father to work in a mill and still inherit the Garden of Eden?
There was a man who worked in a mill.
The king ordered that millers be brought to him.
Said the man to his father, "Father you stay here and work in the mill in my place, and I will go to work for the king. For if some insults come to the workers, I prefer they fall on me and not you."
Such a man puts his father to work in a mill yet inherits the Garden of Eden.

Jerusalem Talmud Kiddushin 1:7

INTERVIEW

If you are to interview an elderly friend or relative, before the interview, write down on a piece of paper everything you know about the person to be interviewed. Then ask questions!

Possible Interview Questions:

1. Where were you born? _____

2. What is the first thing you remember? _____

3. What machines do we have today that you did not have growing up? _____

4. What did you do for fun? _____

5. What was school like? _____

6. When did you go on your first date? _____

7. How did you meet your husband or wife? _____

8. What are the things you are most proud of? _____

9. What is the biggest problem in getting old? _____

10. What makes you afraid? _____

11. How do you deal with this fear? _____

12. Where do you see yourself in five years? _____

13. Do you like to play games? Which ones? _____

14. Did your parents make you clean your room? _____

It is natural for **old people to** be **despised** by the **general population** when they **can no longer function** as they once did, but sit idle and **have no purpose**. The commandment, "Honor your **father and your mother**" was given specifically for this situation   *(Gur Aryeh Halevi)*...

We hear old people say, "**When we were young** we were told to act like adults. Now that we are old, we are **treated like infants**"   *(Bava Kamma 92b)*...

Honor and respect the aged and saintly scholar whose **physical powers** are broken, equally with the young and vigorous scholar whose physical powers are not broken. The broken **tablets of stone** no less than the whole ones had a place **in the Ark** of the **Covenant**   *(Berachot 8b)*.

Old people: How old is an old person? How can you tell they are old? Do they do anything special that makes them old?

Despised: Hated? Do you hate old people? Are you uncomfortable around old people? If so, why? Why would anyone hate old people? Is there anything special that old people do that "turn off" everyone else?

General population: Who is in the general population? Are you part of the general population? Why would the general population dislike old people?

No longer function: In what ways do they "no longer function?" Does the text mean that old people no longer function physically (they can't run or jump or catch?), mentally (they have trouble speaking or thinking or remembering?), or emotionally (they get angry or happy for no reason?).

Have no purpose: What does it mean to "have a purpose in life? Do you have a purpose in life? Do your parent(s) have a purpose in life? If so, what is it? Do old people have a purpose in life? What could it be?

Father and mother: This is one of the Ten Commandments. Why is it such an important commandment? Why would old people be included in this commandment?

When we were young: Were old people ever young? Can you imagine what the old people you know were like when they were younger? How does it feel to be "young?"

Treated like infants: How are old people treated like infants? How are infants treated? How would you feel if you were treated like a baby?

Physical powers: What kind of physical powers would a wise person have?

Tablets of stone: This is the first set of the Ten Commandments.

In the Ark: Why would it be important for both sets of commandments to be in the Ark? What was so special about the Ark?

Texts on L'hader Pnai Zaken: Respect for Elders

It is natural for **old people to** be **despised** by the **general population** when they **can no longer function** as they once did, but sit idle and **have no purpose**. The commandment, "Honor your **father and your mother**" was given specifically for this situation   *(Gur Aryeh Halevi)...*

We hear old people say, "**When we were young** we were told to act like adults. Now that we are old, we are **treated like infants**   *(Bava Kamma 92b)...*

Honor and respect the aged and saintly scholar whose **physical powers** are broken, equally with the young and vigorous scholar whose physical powers are not broken. The broken **tablets of stone** no less than the whole ones had a place **in the Ark** of the **Covenant**   *(Berachot 8b).*

Old people: _____

_____

Despised: _____

_____

_____

General population: _____

_____

No longer function: _____

_____

_____

_____

Have no purpose: _____

_____

_____

Father and mother: _____

_____

When we were young: _____

_____

Treated like infants: _____

_____

Physical powers: _____

Tablets of stone: _____

In the Ark: _____

Thoughts from Danny Siegel

My favorite statistic:

In the first full year of his Eden Alternative at Chase Memorial Nursing Home, a residence for 80 elders in New Berlin, New York, Dr. Thomas reduced the cost of medication from $220,000 to $135,091.

No one dies at Chase. Well, that isn't exactly true. What is true is that no one dies at Chase Memorial Nursing Home for the wrong reasons. The wrong reasons make up a long, long list, a scary list, a list sad with too few people to say, "This has got to stop."

At Chase there are more than 100 birds at the home, most of them living in the rooms of the elders. Two dogs, including Target, a retired racing greyhound destined for Death Row until rescued, and a plain old mutt with a warm and friendly personality named Ginger. There are four cats including Chase and Sanborn. There are many, many children, who attend a summer camp on the grounds…Infants and little and middle-size children everywhere…Plants, gardens, light…

People at Eden have a 15% lower mortality rate than residents of other nursing homes. Nurses aide turnover is slower by 26%. Medications are reduced by half in one year. Infections are 50% less than in other places.

Good People pp. 54-55

Questions

1. How much money did Dr. Thomas save on medication in his first year? _____
   _____

2. What are some of the "wrong reasons" to die at a nursing home? _____
   _____

3. Why would a person look at a nursing home and say, "This has got to stop!" _____
   _____

4. Why is it important for nursing home residents to have animals? _____
   _____

5. Why is it important for children to be around nursing homes? _____
   _____

6. Have you ever visited a nursing home? _____
   _____

7. What did you see there that bothered you? _____

PK BEVILLE: Second Wind Dreams

Life in a nursing home can be pretty bad. We have all visited nursing homes—maybe you went to see a grandparent or, perhaps, your Hebrew School class visited at Hanukkah and sang some songs to the elders gathered around. However you got there, you probably don't remember really enjoying the visit. It is usually pretty depressing, even if they have some birds or other animals as permanent residents. However they try to make residents comfortable and feel at home, the truth is this—you are not at home, at least not at the one where you spent most of your life. And, not only that. You have to rely on someone to get you whatever you might want. It could be something as simple as a radio of your own or maybe a new watch with big numbers that you can read. What if you really enjoyed baking chocolate chip cookies in your own kitchen? It is not likely you can do that in this new place you call "home."

This is where PK Beville comes in. PK's work took her to nursing homes on a regular basis. She spent a lot of time visiting homes and always saw many, many sad and lonely elders. PK was upset—she began to think about the fact that these people had probably raised families, worked long and hard for years to support themselves and their family, and now had lost their independence and had to rely on others for most of their needs. It just wasn't fair!

How could PK make a difference? How could we all make a difference? That is how Second Wind Dreams (SWD) came about. Surely most anyone in a nursing home has some dream, some special wish that they would love to have filled. This is not limited only to elders for there are many young people living in nursing homes because they are disabled and their family cannot care for them at home.

Second Wind Dreams is PK's organization; it is dedicated to making dreams come true for people living in nursing homes. Nursing homes all across the United States have joined SWD in this effort. In every SWD home there is someone who is called a dreamweaver, and it is the dreamweaver's job to make dreams come true for the home's residents.

When you hear what some of these dreams are, you really understand just how important PK's program is. Here are some examples:

1. One woman wanted a cup holder for her wheelchair so she could sip her Ensure while moving about the home.
2. One man remembered how much he loved to go to baseball games. The dreamweaver in his home arranged for tickets to an Atlanta Braves game, a limousine ride to the game, and a visit to the clubhouse to top it off!
3. One woman remembered how much she loved to play the piano. That dreamweaver arranged for a trip to the local Steinway showroom where a beautiful concert piano was waiting. Oh, the beautiful music that was made that day!

For some, the dreams are big, like arranging the visit of a relative you haven't seen in many years. Or, there was Wayne Mix, a man who wanted to visit Sea World and swim with the dolphins!

The truth is, the vast majority of these dreams cost less than $25.00! Such a small price for such big smiles and happiness.

Questions on PK Beville

1. What are the conditions like in many nursing homes? _____
   _____

2. Why are residents of nursing homes likely to be depressed? _____
   _____

3. What are some of the obstacles nursing home residents face to be independent? _____
   _____

4. What made PK upset over the conditions at the nursing homes? _____
   _____

5. What type of organization did PK become involved in? What do they do? _____
   _____

6. What are some of the dreams of nursing home residents? _____
   _____

7. How easy would it be to make these dreams come true? _____
   _____

8. Would you need any special skills to make these dreams come true? _____
   _____

9. What talents do you have that might be used to make dreams come true? _____
   _____

Things To Do

1. Visit a nursing home in your area. Compare it to the description of the Chase Nursing Home.
   How do they differ?

2. See the film, "Gefilte Fish," which talks about three different generations' approach to the issue of
   making gefilte fish.

3. Establish a flower committee to take leftover flowers from the synagogue and other Jewish
   communal events to shelters, hospitals, or residences for the elderly.

4. Ask if your local zoo will bring pets to old-age residences for visiting.

5. Invite an older person to be interviewed by the class about issues that affect elderly people.

6. Call your grandparents or another elderly person and interview them about their lives.
   Present your findings to the class.

7. Ask your congregation if they have a collection of large print prayerbooks for services. Do they have
   a special system in place that makes it easier for people who are hard of hearing to enjoy
   the services?

Ask the following questions:

1. Does your congregation have flowers in the sanctuary on Shabbat? _____

2. Who donates the flowers? Who arranges it?_____

3. What happens to the flowers after services? _____

4. Who decides what happens to them? _____

Action:

1. Go to the person/organization (such as Sisterhood) and ask permission to get the flowers on Sunday mornings.

2. Arrange for use of the congregation kitchen or a room to prepare the flowers into bouquets (three to five flowers each)

3. Arrange the flowers in bouquets (using plastic wrap) and put them in a refrigerator.

4. Write and decorate a card for each bouquet. In the card tell the person who is getting the flowers that you are thinking of them and you hope they feel better this week.

5. Have someone deliver the bouquets to:

   A congregant who has been sick.

   A congregant who is a shut in.

   A congregant who has recently celebrated a simcha.

   A congregant who might just need some cheering up.

   OR

   Ask the rabbi or congregation office to provide the class with a list of people who are ill at home or shut in, or had a simcha (happy occasion) that week. Ask one person from the class to have their parents drive them to the houses/apartments and deliver the flowers.

Now that you have completed these lessons, we have chosen one story to sum up what we hope you have learned from this text/workbook. It is an old story which teaches us about how even the most learned and famous people can refuse to see simple truths. We ask you to read the story and learn from it.

Rabbi Ya'akov Yitzchak was one day walking on the road and came across a peasant whose cart full of straw had overturned.

"Greetings, brother, the peasant cried.

Come help me right my cart."

The rabbi looked at the cart with its thick solid wooden walls and its heavy wooden wheels. He shook his head.

"I'd like to help you but I can't. I'm not strong enough."

He turned to go, but the peasant shouted.

"You can, but you don't want to."

Rabbi Ya'akov Yitzchak was stunned by these harsh words and determined to prove the peasant wrong. He took off his coat and together with the peasant went into the nearby woods to cut saplings for levers.

They hitched the horse to the side of the cart, put the poles beneath the side and began to lift. At a word from the peasant, the horse began to pull and then heave.

Nothing happened at first. Then little by little, their combined efforts began to tell.

Slowly the wagon began to turn, and then in a little while they had it on its wheels.

In silence the two men collected the spilled straw and loaded it back on the wagon.

They set off in the same direction and as they went, the Rabbi asked,

"Brother, how did you know that I could help you?"

The peasant laughed.

"I didn't know any more than you knew that your efforts would fail."

"How did you know that I didn't want to help you?"

"That's easy. I knew you didn't want to because you didn't try."

As told by Martin Buber

At the beginning of this course of study, we told you about

the four questions Danny Siegel asks of everyone.

They are:

1. What am I good at?

2. What do I like to do?

3. Whom do I know?

4. Why not?

We now ask you to add one more question to this list:

What makes you angry? What issues specifically?

Then, when you have answered this question, we ask for the last time this year

GIVEN WHAT YOU HAVE LEARNED,
WHAT WOULD DANNY DO?

_____

_____

_____

_____

_____

_____

_____

About Danny Siegel

Danny Siegel is a well-known author, lecturer, and poet who has spoken in more than 200 North American Jewish communities, to synagogues, JCC's, Federations, and other communal organizations on Tzedakah and Jewish values, besides reading from his own poetry. He is the author of 25½ books on such topics as Mitzvah heroes and practical and personalized Tzedakah, and has produced an anthology of 500 selections of Talmudic quotes about living the Jewish life well called *Where Heaven and Earth Touch.*

Siegel is sometimes referred to as "The Most Famous Unknown Jewish Poet in America"—among his not-well-enough-known poetry books are *A Hearing Heart* and *Unlocked Doors*—as well as *The World's Greatest Expert on Microphilanthropy; The Feeling Person's Thinker;* and *The Pied Piper of Tzedakah.* His volume *Healing: Readings and Meditations* combines poetry and prose and classical Jewish texts for those in need of healing words.

His most recent books in prose include *1 + 1 = 3 and 37 Other Mitzvah Principles For a Meaningful Life; Heroes and Miracle Workers; and Good People,* collections of essays about everyday people who are Mitzvah heroes and great Menschen; *Tell Me a Mitzvah,* Tzedakah stories for children ages 7–12; and *The Humongous Pushka in the Sky,* a storybook for young children.

Ziv Tzedakah Fund, the non-profit Mitzvah organization he founded in 1981, has distributed more than $4,600,000 to worthy individuals and projects.

Danny has a B.S. in Comparative Literature from Columbia University's School of General Studies, and a Bachelor's and Master's of Hebrew Literature from the Jewish Theological Seminary of America.

He is one of three recipients of the prestigious 1993 Covenant Award for Exceptional Jewish Educators.